Native American History

An Enthralling Overview of the Cherokee, Chickasaw, Choctaw, Creek, and Seminole Tribes along with the Trail of Tears

Free limited time bonus

Stop for a moment. We have a free bonus set up for you. The problem is this: we forget 90% of everything that we read after 7 days. Crazy fact, right? Here's the solution: we've created a printable, 1-page pdf summary for this book that you're reading now. All you have to do to get your free pdf summary is to go to the following website:

https://livetolearn.lpages.co/enthrallinghistory/

Once you do, it will be intuitive. Enjoy, and thank you!

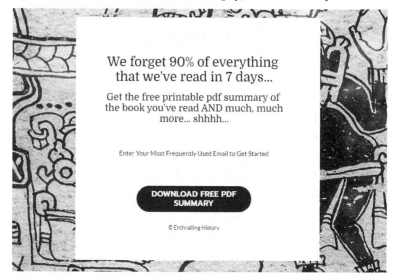

Table of Contents

PART 1: NATIVE AMERICAN TRIBES 1

INTRODUCTION 2

SECTION ONE: THE CIVILIZED TRIBES 4

CHAPTER 1: CHEROKEE 5

CHAPTER 2: CHOCTAW 13

CHAPTER 3: CHICKASAW 19

CHAPTER 4: SEMINOLE 24

CHAPTER 5: MUSCOGEE CREEK 30

CHAPTER 6: OTHER TRIBES 35

SECTION TWO: TRAILS AND TRIBULATIONS 44

CHAPTER 7: ANDREW JACKSON AND MARTIN VAN BUREN 45

CHAPTER 8: INDIAN REMOVAL ACT OF 1830 51

CHAPTER 9: THE TREATY OF NEW ECHOTA 55

CHAPTER 10: THE TRAIL OF TEARS 59

SECTION THREE: RESISTANCE AND OPPOSITION 64

CHAPTER 11: TIPPECANOE AND THE EARLY CREEK WARS 65

CHAPTER 12: THE SEMINOLE TRILOGY AND THE BLACK
HAWK WAR 71

CHAPTER 13: SAND CREEK MASSACRE AND RED CLOUD'S
WAR 75

CHAPTER 14: THE BATTLE OF THE LITTLE BIGHORN AND
WOUNDED KNEE 80

SECTION FOUR: FREEDOM AT WHAT COST? 86

CHAPTER 15: THE FREEDMEN OF THE FIVE TRIBES 87

CHAPTER 16: LEGACY AND HISTORIOGRAPHY 91

CONCLUSION 94

PART 2: TRAIL OF TEARS 96

INTRODUCTION 97

CHAPTER 1: THE FIVE CIVILIZED TRIBES 98

CHAPTER 2: SINISTER ORIGINS 106

CHAPTER 3: THE INDIAN REMOVAL ACT 1830: CAUSE AND
CONSEQUENCE 112

CHAPTER 4: SEMINOLE RESISTANCE: THIS MEANS WAR 118

CHAPTER 5: MANIFEST DESTINY: JACKSON, VAN BUREN, AND
THE TREATY OF NEW ECHOTA 122

CHAPTER 6: ATTACKING THE MUSCOGEE (CREEK) 130

CHAPTER 7: THE ORIGINAL DEATH MARCH? THE TRAIL OF
TEARS 134

CHAPTER 8: LEGAL IMPLICATIONS AND REBUILDING THE
CHEROKEE TRIBE 143

CHAPTER 9: HISTORICAL LEGACY 148

CHAPTER 10: LEGENDARY FIGURES 155

CHAPTER 11: NATIVE AMERICAN REMOVAL: A TIMELINE 172

CONCLUSION 181

AFTERWORD 182

HERE'S ANOTHER BOOK BY ENTHRALLING HISTORY
THAT YOU MIGHT LIKE 186

FREE LIMITED TIME BONUS 187

BIBLIOGRAPHY 188

Part 1: Native American Tribes

An Enthralling Guide to the Cherokee, Chickasaw, Choctaw, Creek, and Seminole

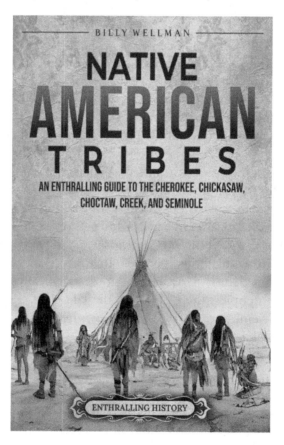

Introduction

The phrase "History of Native Americans" can be misleading. For instance, consider the name "Native Americans." This should surely include all indigenous peoples of the great landmasses of North and South America. However, "Native American" often doesn't include the civilizations of Central America and the Yucatan Peninsula—the Mayan, Olmec, and Aztec. This name does not encompass the various groups that lived and still live in the Andes Mountains or the vast Amazon Basin. "Native American" can also mean the Inuit peoples of the frozen north and native Hawaiians. For our purposes, "Native American" refers exclusively to the indigenous peoples that lived in what is now the continental United States of America. More specifically, we are focusing primarily on five peoples: the Cherokee, the Choctaw, the Chickasaw, the Creek, and the Seminole. In past centuries, these have been called the "Five Civilized Tribes."

This name is, of course, misleading. What earlier scholars were trying to say by giving these tribes the "civilized" moniker is that they attempted to adopt the hallmarks of American society. These Native Americans would don suits and dresses, speak English, and convert to Christianity. The men cut their hair short, and the families lived in permanent settlements where they focused on agriculture. Some of them also owned slaves. This was, for earlier scholars, what made them civilized and set them apart from tribes that continued to dress in traditional clothes and live in semi-permanent villages where they worshiped their own gods and spoke their own languages.

One of the criteria for civilization in the Western mind is writing. Writing, it is believed, sets civilized man apart from animals. Many Native Americans did not have a tradition of writing. They did not have alphabets, and it was believed they did not have records of their own history, though this would turn out to be incorrect.

One of the greatest problems for European colonists in understanding Native Americans was the failure to realize they had entered a world that had recently been turned upside down. Before English colonists had landed in Jamestown and Plymouth Rock Plantation, the Native American population had been rocked by war, famine, and disease. The invasion of Europeans in Central America caused waves of change to ripple throughout the entire world. An exchange had begun that continues today—the exchange of people, ideas, goods, flora, and fauna, both seen and invisible. For Native Americans, this time seemed like it might be the end of the world—and, in many ways, it was. Their world as it had existed before the European colonies were gone. They were, therefore, faced with a choice to fight, assimilate, or retreat from the spread of Europeans. The Five Civilized Tribes chose all three at various times. They allied with one European power to fight another. They fought against and for American leaders. They fought on battlefields and in courtrooms. Some tried to become part of American society, building schools to teach their children how to look, behave, and sound like Americans. They moved many times, both independently and as part of forced migrations. Today, many of them are trying to save their traditional cultures, languages, and religions.

This book will attempt to tell their story, the story of those five tribes. It will not go back into the distant past, and it will not be able to cover modern issues within the Native American community. But it will tell the story of how a group of people dealt with a world that had suddenly and drastically changed—and continued to change—and how they dealt with these changes as Native Americans.

SECTION ONE:
THE CIVILIZED TRIBES

Chapter 1: Cherokee

The Cherokee Nation was originally part of a larger culture now called the Mississippian culture. This culture, which existed throughout the Midwest and Southeastern United States, was notable for large cities with central flat-topped earthen pyramids. There, sacred people lived, and temples were built. One of the largest cities was Cahokia, which is in modern-day Illinois. That city, which peaked in the 1200s CE, had an estimated population of over 70,000. However, the Mississippian culture would soon be decimated by an invisible invader.

It began, perhaps surprisingly, 4,500 miles away from the Mississippi River Valley in 1500 CE when a child named Hernando de Soto was born, just eight years after Columbus had sailed to the New World for Spain. De Soto grew up with dreams of following in Columbus' footsteps, so when he was old enough, he traveled to the West Indies and made a name for himself as a good soldier. He was made second in command of Francisco Pizarro's expedition to conquer what would become Peru. In 1536, de Soto returned to Spain as a wealthy man and settled in Seville.

However, de Soto soon became restless, and on May 25th, 1539, he landed with 700 men in Florida. They traveled north into what would become the state of Alabama and met serious resistance from Native Americans. They then went west to the Mississippi, becoming the first Europeans to travel on that river. De Soto and his men met numerous thriving Native American populations. They traveled to North Carolina and, at a place called Xualla, met the Tsalagi people, known today as the Cherokee. The Tsalagi gave de Soto food and gifts, and he went on his way, looking for gold in the Appalachian Mountains. He and his men, however, left something behind that neither they nor the Tsalagi were aware of—disease. Due to the introduction of European diseases like smallpox and scarlet fever, Native American populations in North America plummeted starting in 1500. By 1600, the Mississippian cities had been abandoned, and the people were scattered into confederacies of small villages or kinship groups. The Tsalagi continued, but their numbers dwindled. De Soto himself was struck with a fever and died in 1542, his party having been reduced by half due to battle with Native Americans and disease.

According to Cherokee tradition, their people had originally lived in a land of constant flooding. Wanting to escape this, they attempted to build a house that would reach heaven. The gods destroyed part of their tower, but they continued to build. The gods destroyed it again, and this time they decided to move out of the flooded area. They traveled from their old country to a new land. The journey took many years, and their path was obscured when water covered it. In their new land, they found abundant places to grow corn and other crops and hunt for meat. Their tribe consisted of seven clans, and they had seven key towns among many dozen.

By the middle of the seventeenth century, after the collapse of the large Mississippian cities, the Cherokee had become the largest nation in the Southeast. They occupied 40,000 square miles in western North Carolina and eastern Tennessee.

The Cherokee Nation was primarily a confederation of towns, and a council of "Beloved Men" governed each town. Women enjoyed a high status and could become political leaders. The Cherokee were farmers who grew corn, beans, melons, tobacco, and sunflowers; they hunted for their meat and could forage in the abundant forests when crops failed. A visitor in the early eighteenth century would have first come upon the "town fields" where the whole population worked together. The crops from these fields were kept by the chief and used for visitors, the poor, and emergencies. As the visitor walked into the heart of the town, they would pass through a defensive blockade made of wooden poles. Within this wall were individual dwellings. Cherokee homes typically consisted of four buildings: a kitchen, store room, and winter and summer living quarters. These were of wattle and daub construction since the Cherokee had not yet been introduced to iron axes. In the center of the town was a square of hard-packed soil surrounded by four buildings used for meetings with the town council. In this area, the community held rituals and festivals, and in the very center was a fire.

The Cherokee had a complicated religious belief system. One element was the symbolism of cardinal directions. For the Cherokee, East was associated with the color red and success, North with blue and defeat, West with black and death, and South with white and purity. They held to a strong belief in the idea that white was pure and represented happiness. This would factor into how they treated the new white visitors among them. They believed that the light complexion of these strangers meant that they should be approached peacefully and as honored guests. It was therefore quite confusing for many Cherokee when the whites who visited them in the early eighteenth century did not seem to be creatures of purity and peace but actually creatures of war.

The French later had dealings with the Cherokee, but it would be the British who secured an official relationship with the tribe. In 1729, the Carolina colony was handed over to the Crown and was split into North and South Carolina. Charles Town, in South Carolina, had become a busy port dealing in the trade of rice, indigo, and slaves. In this British colony, a plantation system that relied on enslaved Africans had developed. In fact, slaves now outnumbered the colonists. Before this, there had been a Native American slave trade in which the Cherokee captured people from other tribes and handed them over to the British in exchange for tools, guns, and gunpowder. The Native American slaves were then shipped from Charles Town to the Caribbean to work on plantations. The Native American slave trade had mostly died out after a war from 1715 to 1717 with the Yamasee tribe and several allies, including the Cherokee. The Cherokee continued to trade with the British in the Virginia and Carolina colonies, but there was no official treaty between them. It was in the year 1729 that Sir Alexander Cuming, 2nd Baronet, stepped onto the docks of Charles Town with a mission in mind.

Cuming was a Scottish nobleman whose family fortune was all but gone. According to his account, he had decided to go to South Carolina because of his wife's dream. What exactly drove him to make the arduous journey into the heart of the Cherokee Nation is unknown. He was not, as he told the Cherokee, an official representative of the King of England. He, in fact, had no authority to establish agreements between the Cherokee and England, but that is exactly what he did. The Cherokee, at that time, were grouped into three main areas: the Overhill towns of eastern Tennessee, the middle towns of western North Carolina and northern Georgia, and the lower towns of western South Carolina. Cuming traveled first to the lower towns and charmed the Cherokee, presenting himself as a representative of King George. After traveling to the middle towns, he learned of a Cherokee crown, the Crown of Tannassy, which was made of possum skin dyed yellow or red. He then went on to the Overhill towns to find the crown and take it so that he could lay it at the feet of the king.

Cuming gained the favor of Moytoy of Tellico, who was hoping to succeed the previous leader of the Cherokee, Wrosetasatow, who had recently died. At a meeting in Nikwasi in April of 1730, Cuming declared Moytoy the emperor of all the Cherokee. He then demanded that the Cherokee hand over their crown, sacred eagle feathers, and the scalps of their enemies and pledge allegiance to King George. This worked, and Cuming presented the crown, eagle feathers, scalps, and seven Cherokee to King George in June of 1730. A formal treaty was then drawn up, declaring the Cherokee loyal British subjects. Cuming asked to be made ambassador and overlord of the Cherokee, but this request was denied. Cuming would later end up in debtor's prison, then Jamaica, and would write his memoir before his death in 1775.

Moytoy was soon killed in battle. The British tried to put his son in place as emperor of the Cherokee, but the Cherokee were not used to a single ruler, and leadership roles were not inherited— they were earned. Moytoy's son was usurped by a leader named Connecorte, or Old Hop. Still, the Cherokee did not recognize one single ruler over the entire tribe. One Cherokee town might make an agreement with the English, while another town might make a separate agreement with the French. The English could view this as treachery, but it was inconsequential to the Cherokee, as each town or group of towns was at liberty to do whatever was best for them.

Trade became a key feature in Cherokee life in the mid-1700s. They did not make the weapons they used to hunt or their clothes; they had to rely on trade to obtain these things. Typically, they traded furs for items, primarily from the British. To get a single rifle, the Cherokee had to provide seven buck skins or fourteen does. The price for a blanket was three buck skins, and a pair of shoes cost two buck skins. The Cherokee complained that the prices were too high, but the British traders claimed the prices were too low. The British hoped to leverage their position to obtain ever more furs from the Cherokee—and use the Cherokee to make things hard on their enemies, the French and Spanish.

While the Europeans manipulated the Native Americans, the Cherokee were internally competing with each other for power. One of the most powerful among the Cherokee was *Attakullakulla*, or "Little Carpenter," who had been among the Cherokee that Alexander Cuming had brought to London to see the king. Little Carpenter had spent several years as a prisoner among the Ottawa. Upon his return to his homeland, he seemed to believe the best interest of the Cherokee was to continue their uneasy alliance with Great Britain, which he believed would win in the upcoming war between the French and English.

Ten years after Alexander Cuming's journey into the Cherokee Nation, there was an outbreak of smallpox, reportedly killing off half of their population in a matter of months. Many of the Cherokee took it as a sign of divine retribution. The French tried to use this to sow discord between the Cherokee and the English. They sent an agent who told the Cherokee that the English had spread the disease on purpose. The English were concerned. The Cherokee represented a defensive buffer between them and the Native Americans allied with the French. By 1755, the English had agreed to build forts to help protect the Cherokee. In exchange, the Cherokee would provide warriors for their battles with the French. The most well-known fort was Fort Prince George in northwest South Carolina along the Keowee River.

Peace did not last long. In 1758, the Virginia militia attacked Moytoy in retaliation for the supposed theft of some horses. Moytoy, in return, led raids against the English. This was the beginning of the Anglo-Cherokee War, which would last from 1758 to 1761. This conflict was in the midst of the larger war known today as the French and Indian War that lasted from 1754 to 1763.

The Cherokee had begun the French and Indian War as allies to the English; however, the French had been courting the Cherokee leaders for some time. Old Hop, now a very old man, was pro-French, as were other leaders such as Raven, Mankiller, and Old Hop's nephew, Standing Turkey. After Moytoy had led attacks against the British, sixteen Cherokee prisoners were killed at Fort Prince George. The Cherokee then attacked and killed the garrison at Fort Loudon near the powerful Cherokee city of Chota. Also in 1758, several Cherokee, after helping the British attack the French Fort Duquesne, were killed by Virginia militiamen after a misunderstanding involving some horses.

In 1759, the Cherokee declared open war on the British. The British immediately stopped supplying the Cherokee with gunpowder. In response, the Cherokee sent twenty-nine chiefs to negotiate, but these representatives were taken prisoner and kept at Fort Prince George. The Cherokee continued to attack British settlements and stormed Fort Prince George to rescue the prisoners. They killed the fort commander, but his replacement had all the prisoners massacred. The Cherokee continued to raid settlements, going into North Carolina as well. An army of 1,200 British soldiers was sent to stop the Cherokee, but they were defeated. The Cherokee then took Fort Loudon.

In 1761, a new British army of 2,600 men defeated the Cherokee at Echoee Pass and then destroyed fifteen Cherokee towns. Upon their defeat, the Cherokee removed Standing Turkey from power; Old Hop had died years earlier. In his place as the "First Beloved Man" was Attakullakulla (Little Carpenter), who was decidedly pro-British. The Cherokee signed a peace treaty with Virginia and also with South Carolina.

To verify that hostilities had ended for all Cherokee, the Virginia Colony sent a man named Henry Timberlake across the Appalachian Mountains and into the Cherokee Overhill towns to deliver copies of the treaty to the "beloved men" (chiefs) in those towns. Timberlake stayed as a personal guest of the Cherokee chief Ostenaco for several months. He kept a record of his experience which survives to this day. In it, Timberlake explains that in the dark and smoky confines of what he calls the "townhouse," Ostenaco explained that the bloody tomahawk that had been raised against the English would now be buried deep in the ground, never to be raised again. Timberlake, Ostenaco, and all the people gathered in the town-house—which Timberlake believed could have sat 500 people—and smoked the peace pipes that were passed around. Timberlake's time with the Cherokee was fraught with tension because rumors were coming in that the English had killed more Cherokee, but Ostenaco kept calm and said he would only believe the news if it came from a credible source. Attakullakulla was set to arrive, but before he did, a group of warriors returned with four scalps they had obtained in a battle with Shawnee, including at least one French soldier. It seemed the Cherokee would remain allies of the British. However, the situation continued to be troubled all the way to the American Revolution.

In March of 1775, Attakullakulla and other chiefs agreed to sell a large portion of their lands to the Transylvania Company run by Richard Henderson, a land speculator who hoped to create a new colony. This land, which would become a large part of Kentucky and middle Tennessee, amounted to twenty million acres north of the Cumberland River and south of the Ohio River. In exchange, the Cherokee were given about 10,000 British pounds of goods they desperately needed. This Transylvania Colony would be short-lived. The Virginia Assembly and Continental Congress refused to recognize Henderson's claim since he had failed to get permission to make the sale in the first place. He had agents, most notably Daniel Boone, scouting the area for ten years before the purchase, but instead, Virginia took the portion of Kentucky and made it part of its colony.

Attakullakulla's son, Dragging Canoe, saw the sale of so much of their land as a betrayal against his people. This new generation felt that the Anglo-Americans would destroy the Cherokee, just like the tribes of New England and Virginia. Dragging Canoe felt that Native Americans should abandon the ways of white people, including Christianity, and fight against the spread and oppression of the whites in their land.

When the American Revolution came, Dragging Canoe and many others broke from the Cherokee and allied themselves with the British. They attacked American settlements, and the Americans attacked Cherokee villages in return. Many Cherokee became displaced, and Dragging Canoe led them to new settlements on Chickamauga Creek. They were soon joined by other Cherokee, Creek, Tories, and escaped Black slaves. This group was called the Chickamauga. Americans then attacked these settlements while most of the warriors were away fighting for the British. Instead of trying to rebuild, Dragging Canoe formed five new settlements along the Tennessee River. About this time, John Donelson was leading a group of women and children on flatboats to an area he had purchased from Richard Henderson that would become Nashville, Tennessee. Donelson's daughter, Rachel, was with him. The Chickamauga attacked the flatboats as they progressed down the river, killing many of the party. Rachel survived the ordeal and went on to marry a young man named Andrew Jackson, the future President of the United States.

In 1785, the Cherokee chief Corn Tassel signed the Treaty of Hopewell, which established boundaries between the new United States of America and the Cherokee lands and promised that no whites would settle on their land. But the relationship between the Cherokee and the Americans remained contentious, and crimes were committed on both sides. The Cherokee ceded land to the US government in exchange for annuities and goods.

In 1821, the Cherokee had their own alphabet, and many Cherokee learned to read and write quickly. By 1828, they had their own newspaper, the *Cherokee Phoenix.*

The Americans began to pressure the Cherokee into moving from their homelands and emigrating to lands west of the Mississippi River, but the Cherokee were divided on the idea. However, in 1835, 500 Cherokee claiming to represent their entire nation signed a treaty at New Echota that established the forced removal of the Cherokee in exchange for $5 million and land in modern-day Oklahoma. At first, only 2,000 Cherokee voluntarily left. The federal government then sent 7,000 troops to force the remainder of the Cherokee to travel the 1,200 miles of what would be called the Trail of Tears. Along the way, an estimated 25 percent died from disease, starvation, and exhaustion.

In the late nineteenth century, Cherokee shamans and cultural leaders began to collect their nation's various stories, proverbs, wisdom, and medicine in a way that could be shared with the outside world. White scholars like James Mooney lived among the Cherokee and learned from native Cherokee such as Swimmer (Ayunini) the shaman, John Ax, Gahuni, and others about the rich cultural heritage of the Cherokee.

Chapter 2: Choctaw

Before they were forced to go west, the Choctaw lived in southwestern Alabama and southern Mississippi. Like the Cherokee, during the seventeenth and eighteenth centuries, they were caught between the growing powers of Spain, France, and England and competing with their neighboring tribes like the Creek and Chickasaw. When Europeans arrived in Choctaw country, it was not a particular shock to the tribe because their lore said that the Creator had breathed life into many different pairs of first humans. The Europeans were seen as just another group given life by the Creator.

Before the arrival of Europeans, agriculture was already an important part of the Choctaw's daily life. They often grew surpluses of corn and traded with other tribes and then European settlers. They were involved in the Native American slave trade and traded furs, corn, and other crops for cloth, guns, alcohol, and tools. The European traders often married Choctaw women, and their offspring, considered "half-bloods," were often literate, educated, and spoke both a European language and their native tongue. This led to them occupying many positions of power within Choctaw society.

Some of the Choctaw entered into the agricultural market of the European colonies, especially the British, losing almost all of their Native American heritage in the process. The cooperation of Choctaw leaders was often bought with cash and gifts, and missionaries regularly tried to convert them to Christianity and convince them to adopt a more European lifestyle. The Choctaw had already copied the Europeans in one way: as early as 1720, they began to own Black slaves.

Like many Native Americans in the Southeast, the Choctaw enjoyed sports, especially stickball, or *Ishtaboli*, which is still played today. The sport has few rules, and games can feature almost limitless players and last for days. It features a ball, or *Towa*, made of leather strips, which is handled using sticks with cups (*Kapucha*) that the players use to try and hit goalposts at either end of the field. This game was historically used to settle disputes between tribes and families. It also kept warriors in fighting condition.

The Choctaw first allied with the French in 1729 to annihilate the Natchez, a neighboring tribe. The Natchez were originally part of the Quigualtam chiefdom de Soto met in 1542 or 1543. After their population loss from European diseases, the Natchez formed into five settlement districts known as Flour, Jenzenaque, White Apple, Grigra, and Tiou. Like the Choctaw, the Natchez were farmers, hunters, and warriors who enjoyed stickball. In the 1720s, the English turned the Natchez against the French. The Natchez rose against the French but were defeated by an alliance of other tribes, including the Choctaw, Cherokee, Creek, and Chickasaw. The Natchez were decimated and forced to leave their homeland.

However, the French would lose the French and Indian War in 1763, and the Choctaw would suffer for their allegiance to the French. The British took some of the Choctaw lands in Mississippi, and some of the tribe opted to go further west in search of more land. Still, many of the Choctaw remained prosperous due to their focus on farming and trade. They continued to own large tracts of land, from which they could sell crops and livestock to other tribes and European settlers.

However, the formation of the United States created new challenges for the Choctaw. In January of 1786, the Choctaw at the foothills of the Smoky Mountains signed the Treaty of Hopewell with representatives of the United States. The treaty's provisions were the cessation of some land and a promise of perpetual peace. It was agreed that no Americans would settle on Choctaw land and that any Americans who committed a crime against any Choctaw would be punished. The United States awarded protection to the tribe. The boundaries between the two were set, and the Choctaw agreed to inform the US if anyone was planning to open hostilities against the Americans. The continuing problem was that Americans were increasingly covetous of Choctaw land, and the government was constantly under pressure to take more and more land from the Native American tribes of the Southeast.

Chief Pushmataha.

In 1798, the Mississippi Territory was created, and in 1800, President Thomas Jefferson made it clear that he wanted the US to control all the land east of the Mississippi River, including all of the Choctaw's homeland. As a result, the tribe had to negotiate control of their lands with American agents. In 1801, the Choctaw signed the Treaty of Fort Adams, ceding almost three million acres of land to the US government. The following year, they signed the Treaty of Fort Confederation, which added another 10,000 acres to US land. The next year, it was the Treaty of Hoe Buckintoopa. Then, in 1805, they signed the Treaty of Mount Dexter, ceding over four million acres.

One of the treaty signers was Pushmataha, also known as the "Indian General." Pushmataha was one of the three regional chiefs of the Choctaw during the 19th century and is often considered the greatest of the Choctaw chiefs. His name is often translated as "messenger of death," and he was well-known among the Choctaw for his abilities as a fighter and hunter.

In 1811, the Shawnee chief Tecumseh was touring Choctaw villages, attempting to persuade them to join his coalition of Native Americans to ally with the British and fight against the Americans in what would become the War of 1812. Pushmataha rejected Tecumseh's proposal, bringing him to the attention of the American government, which reached out to Pushmataha as a potential ally. The "Red Stick" Creek had attacked the Americans at Fort Mims, and Pushmataha saw this as a chance to gather the Choctaw and fight against their old enemy, the Creek. In 1813, Pushmataha was made a captain in the American army and formed a battalion of volunteer Choctaw to aid the Americans in defeating the Creek and the British. He was then promoted to lieutenant colonel. Pushmataha and his men defeated the Creek at the Battle of Econachaca, also called Holy Ground, in December 1813 and again along the Tombigbee River in 1814. His success brought him much acclaim, and he was eventually promoted to brigadier general.

Once the War of 1812 concluded and the British and Tecumseh's alliance were defeated, Pushmataha returned to his homeland to represent the Choctaw people. Under direct threats from President Andrew Jackson, Pushmataha and other chiefs signed the Treaty of Doak's Stand in 1820, which gave up over five million acres—half of the Choctaw land—in exchange for land across the Mississippi River in what would become Arkansas. Pushmataha claimed the land they were receiving was not as good as the land they were giving up. Jackson eventually stated that if they did not accept the terms, their nation would be destroyed. The Choctaw, seeing no better course, were forced to sign the treaty. In 1824, Pushmataha and other chiefs traveled to Washington to express their concerns about the terms of this treaty. Soon after arriving in the capital, Pushmataha fell ill and died on December 24th, exactly eleven years after his famous victory at the Battle of Holy Ground.

Pushmataha was not the only Choctaw leader to die on this trip to Washington. Chief Apukshunnubbee also died of a broken neck after falling off a cliff. The deaths of these two great men crippled the Choctaw's ability to negotiate with Washington, DC. Six years later, the Treaty of Dancing Rabbit Creek was signed. The Choctaw were led by Greenwood LeFlore, a "mixed-blood" Native American who was a member of the Choctaw elite, though he was disliked by the "pure-blood" Choctaw.

LeFlore encouraged the Choctaw to establish permanent settlements, focus on agriculture, convert to Christianity, and send their children to US schools for their education. However, with the election of Andrew Jackson and the eventual passing of the Indian Removal Act, it became obvious that the Choctaw, who could not mount any armed resistance, would be forced to leave their homelands. At Dancing Rabbit Creek, LeFlore explained that many of the Choctaw would leave Mississippi and go west, but he wanted the treaty to state that any Choctaw who chose to stay would be granted land and US citizenship. This was agreed, and the treaty was signed.

The Choctaw then became the first tribe to undergo the long trek from their homelands to the Indian Territory in Oklahoma on the Trail of Tears. The US government did not fulfill its promise to give land and citizenship to the Choctaw that remained in Mississippi. Their land was given away to white settlers, and it would be many years before the Choctaw of Mississippi would receive recognition from the United States. Of the Choctaw who journeyed along the Trail of Tears, many thousands perished along the way.

Before the journey began, a census was taken of those Choctaw traveling west. There were 17,693 Choctaw, 151 whites, and 521 enslaved people. The first group that traveled west under federal supervision was plagued by rain and then a horrid winter. The next group faced cholera outbreaks. By the fall of 1833, 6,000 Choctaw remained in Mississippi and refused to leave. In all, more than 2,500 people died during the emigration. In the late 1830s, the Choctaw Nation in Oklahoma formed a government that mirrored the US government. It had judicial, executive, legislative, and military branches. Only male Choctaws could vote. Four district chiefs made up the executive branch, and the General Council formed the legislative. Women and all people of African descent were barred from voting or holding any offices, which is interesting since women had long held important roles within Choctaw culture and were the primary farmers of their society.

After their removal, the Choctaw had a brief recovery period under their new laws in their new land. Since the early nineteenth century, they had produced cotton and enjoyed its profits. They engaged in large plantation-style farming and used enslaved people like the Southern States. By 1840, enslaved people made up 14 percent of the Choctaw population. The best location for plantations in the Choctaw Nation was along the Red

River of Oklahoma. There, Choctaws such as Robert M. Jones owned several plantations and hundreds of enslaved people. However, Jones' holdings were the exception, not the rule. Most Choctaw farmers owned between ten and twenty acres and primarily practiced subsistence farming. Still, enslaved people in the Choctaw Nation received the same treatment as those in the southern states. The Choctaw instituted laws to stop the spread of abolitionist rhetoric, ban enslaved people from learning to read and write, and keep enslaved people from owning property or carrying a firearm without the permission of their enslaver.

When the Civil War broke out in 1861, the Choctaw ignored suggestions of neutrality and firmly aligned themselves with the Confederacy, though they did not go as far as to make it official. This only made sense since the Choctaw had adopted a lifestyle very much in line with the Southern States. On the other hand, it might seem surprising since the state governments of Mississippi and Alabama had worked so hard to expel them just three decades earlier. In the end, the Choctaw signed a formal treaty with the Confederacy in the summer of 1861 and provided several regiments of Choctaw soldiers, who fought on the side of the Confederacy (as did the Cherokee and the Chickasaw). They believed the Confederacy would recognize their status as a sovereign nation, but the eventual defeat of the Confederate States led to more difficulties for Native Americans.

Chapter 3: Chickasaw

The Chickasaw, who lived in northern Mississippi, northern Alabama, western Tennessee, and western Kentucky, were fewer in number than other tribes, but they became well-known for their prowess as warriors. Like the Choctaw, they spoke the Muskogean language. Some archaeologists argue that the Chickasaw and the Choctaw came from the older Plaquemine culture, which existed primarily in Louisiana as early as 1200 CE.

Like the Cherokee and Choctaw, the Chickasaw were caught between the competing powers of England and France, who supported them in wars against other Native Americans while also helping other tribes battle and raid the Chickasaw. The Europeans quickly adopted the "divide and conquer" strategy in dealing with the Native Americans of the Southeast. The Chickasaw acquired firearms from English traders from South Carolina and then began to attack and raid the Choctaw for captives, which they sold to the colonists. This activity all but stopped once the Choctaw were able to get firearms from the French. In the 18th century, the Chickasaw were often at war with the French and the Choctaw. In 1736, the Chickasaw defeated the French and their Native American allies in two pitched battles when the French attacked the villages of Ogoula Tchetoka and Ackia. Battles with the French continued until the end of the French and Indian War in 1763, when France gave up its regions east of the Mississippi River.

Tecumseh, Shawnee war chief.
https://commons.wikimedia.org/wiki/File:Tecumseh02.jpg

In 1768, a Shawnee boy was born near Chillicothe, Ohio, who would grow up to be the Shawnee Chief Tecumseh. He eventually led a group of warriors to attack settler's flatboats coming down the Ohio River. This was extremely successful. In 1791, under the direction of war chiefs Blue Jacket and Little Turtle, Tecumseh proved himself at the Battle of the Wabash when he led a group of warriors that helped defeat General Arthur St. Clair and his army. But, when he faced the Chickasaw at the Battle of Fallen Timbers in 1794 while they were assisting General Anthony Wayne, Tecumseh was defeated.

The Chickasaw, through pressure from the Americans, attempted to engage in white civilization. They educated their children in schools, converted to Christianity, owned private property, and engaged in agriculture. The idea of "civilizing" these Native American tribes was promoted by Presidents Washington and Jefferson. The general assumption was that once Native Americans adopted white culture, white people would accept them into their society. This would prove to be unfounded, of course. The Chickasaw also signed the Treaty of Hopewell in 1786, which promised peace and cooperation between their nation and the United States.

Like other tribes, the Chickasaw were heavily influenced by so-called "half-bloods." A trader named James Logan Colbert became an adopted Chickasaw in the 18th century. He may have been the son of a white father and Chickasaw mother. James ultimately married three high-ranking Chickasaw women and fathered several sons by each wife. Because inheritance and clan membership were matrilineal, these sons all became powerful leaders, especially because they were raised bilingual. Colbert raised his sons to know the ways of white culture, but they were also taught how to be Chickasaw. One of these sons was Chief George Colbert, also known as *Tootemastubbe*.

George Colbert fought against Tecumseh's forces at the Battle of Fallen Timbers. By 1800, he had established a ferry at Cherokee, Alabama. This ferry proved very successful, as it was across the Tennessee River and along the important trade route of the Natchez Trace. Colbert acquired land and began growing cotton; he owned several slaves. George and his brothers Levi and James negotiated with the US government on behalf of the Chickasaw. In the Creek Wars, Colbert recruited warriors and allied with General Andrew Jackson against the "Red Sticks." He also fought alongside the Americans in the War of 1812. Although Colbert was involved in the negotiations that led to the removal of the Chickasaw from their homeland and placement in the Choctaw lands of Oklahoma, he died along the Trail of Tears before reaching the new Chickasaw reservations.

The Treaty of Tuscaloosa, negotiated between then Senator Andrew Jackson and the Chickasaw, resulted in the loss of a significant portion of the Chickasaw territory in Tennessee and Kentucky. It would be called "Jackson's Purchase" or the Jackson Purchase. Today, this refers only to the portion that lies within the state of Kentucky, but at the time, it included territory in western Tennessee as well.

In 1832, the Chickasaw gave up the rest of their homeland in Mississippi, over 6.2 million acres, in the Treaty of Pontotoc Creek with the United States government. The preamble to this decision was a long history of pressure from the US government, in conjunction with land speculators who wanted all the land east of the Mississippi cleared of Native Americans and opened for white settlement. The proposed land offered to the Chickasaw west of the Mississippi River was deemed unsatisfactory by the Chickasaw, who ventured to inspect the land before signing any treaty. Things were compounded by the appearance of numerous squatters in Chickasaw territory within Mississippi. The state government of Mississippi was also actively attempting to push the Chickasaw out of their land. The Treaty of Pontotoc Creek centered on the agreement that the Chickasaw would give up their territory for suitable land that the US government would find for them, but not land that was already determined.

In 1837, the Chickasaw agreed to buy land from the Choctaw for roughly $500,000 in the Treaty of Doaksville. So, in 1837–1838, 4,914 Chickasaw and 1,156 enslaved people made the trek to their new land west of the Mississippi. The sale of their allotments in Mississippi profited them about $3 million. Their Trail of Tears was perhaps not as traumatic as the Choctaw and Cherokee's; however, it was still accompanied by suffering and loss, negatively affecting the tribe for decades, if not longer.

Once they arrived in what would become Oklahoma, they began the difficult task of rebuilding their society. Holmes Colbert, great-grandson of James Logan Colbert and grandson of James Holmes Colbert, became a prominent leader of the Chickasaw in the mid-19th century and helped to write the Chickasaw constitution. He had been educated in an American school but, like his ancestors, had learned the ways of the Chickasaw as well. He was therefore groomed for a leadership role within his tribe. He married Elizabeth Love, who was also educated in American schools but was Chickasaw. When the American Civil War began, the Chickasaw were the first to ally themselves with the Confederate States. The Chickasaw also sent soldiers to fight against the Union. It is perhaps noteworthy that it was not until the Civil War that the Chickasaw took up arms against English-speaking people—they had previously only fought the French and other Native American tribes.

Not all Chickasaw supported the Confederacy. Notably, the family of the outlaw-turned-politician, Fred Tecumseh Waite, fled Chickasaw territory during the Civil War because they were known supporters of the Union. Fred was part of Billy the Kid's gang but returned to Chickasaw territory, where he became a representative. He was elected Speaker of the House three times and then became a senator.

After the Civil War ended, the Chickasaw, Choctaw, and Cherokee were forced to emancipate their enslaved population and give up portions of their territory in Oklahoma. The Chickasaw signed a new peace treaty in 1866 with the US government. This treaty required that any freed slaves that wanted to stay in Chickasaw territory would be granted Chickasaw citizenship; if they went to the US, they would become US citizens. Those who were freed and stayed became known as the Chickasaw Freedmen, and many of their descendants still live in Oklahoma today. However, the Chickasaw did not grant them citizenship unless they could prove their parents were of Chickasaw lineage. Because the Chickasaw failed to hold up that portion of the treaty, the US punished them by taking almost half their territory without giving them anything in return.

Chapter 4: Seminole

The Seminole Tribe did not exist until the 18th century when some of the Lower Creek Native Americans in Georgia and Alabama migrated to Florida in response to encroachment from British settlers. However, the label "Creek" is derived from British colonists, who lumped a wide array of tribal people, societies, and towns into this one nation. They all spoke similar languages, including Muscogee, Hitchiti, and Choctaw. The Creek Confederation was broken into two groups, the Upper Creek and the Lower Creek.

This group of Creek divided into clans, which were matrilineal and named after animals or natural forces. Thus, someone of the panther clan might be away from their home village but would find relatives who could help them because they were all of the same clan. Relationships between clans varied, as well. Additionally, there were town councils and various clan camps. Towns or groups of towns might have a chief, sometimes referred to as a *miko*, who could call together meetings and control surplus food supplies in emergencies but otherwise didn't have extraordinary powers. Europeans often assumed the chiefs were like kings and therefore autocratic leaders of a whole nation when this was simply not the case. The British, for example, might convince a chief to sign a treaty and assume this meant the entire tribe would follow his lead; however, this was rarely the case. When Native Americans were required to make large-scale decisions, it often took considerable time to arrange all the councils and come to a consensus. To Europeans, this often had the (false) appearance of stalling or playing political games.

Like the other Native Americans in the area, these Creek grew to rely on trade with Europeans for metal utensils, firearms, cloth, and livestock. The so-called Creek had practiced slavery before the arrival of Europeans, but the European practice of slavery first introduced them to the idea of slaves as property. The relationship between the Creek and eventually the Seminole and slaves of African descent was complicated. Slaves were treated as property but also protected due to their high value. English settlers began complaining about escaped slaves going to Creek villages, where they were taken in and could not be retrieved. This connection became even stronger with the Seminole, who formed close bonds with runaway slaves in their territory and relied on them as interpreters and allies.

As mentioned earlier, in the 18th century, a large contingent of Lower Creek Native Americans left their lands in Alabama and Georgia and traveled into Spanish Florida to escape the expansion of British settlers. The British called them Seminole, from the Spanish word *cimarrones*, which means "wild ones" or "ones that broke away." In central Florida, the Seminole found cattle left by Spanish ranchers and began to raise them. (An early Seminole leader was called "Cowkeeper.") The Seminole developed their own way of life and culture separate from the other Creek tribes. Unlike other tribes that continued to move in search of fur, the Seminole traded primarily in the cattle they had learned to raise so well. By 1789, they were trading primarily with Panton, Leslie & Company, which bought cattle from every Seminole village. The Seminole were fiercely independent but desired peace and trade with the white settlers—as long as there was no attempt to dominate them.

The Seminole of Florida hold that they have lived within the borders of Florida for thousands of years. They contend that they are the original people of Florida, and this may very well be the case. Connected by tradition and kinship to the Mississippian culture, the native population of Florida was continually in flux from the depredation of disease and warfare with Europeans and other tribes, as well as the introduction of new blood in the way of migrating populations from all over the southeastern US.

Seminole, Miccosukee, Muscogee, Calusa, and Creek are all names given to groups of Native Americans at various times and sometimes included the native people of Florida, Georgia, and Alabama. The group we now call the Seminole (who have adopted the name themselves) is surely a mixture of different identities that were bound together and forged into a common consciousness in Florida as they faced the expanding foreign powers around them.

Problems arose at the end of the 18th century through the beginning of the 19th century when competition between England, Spain, and the newly-established United States led to select *mikos* being bribed to cajole their kinsmen into trade alliances with various European and American powers. From this came the so-called "nativist" movement, exemplified by the Shawnee leader Tecumseh, who sent emissaries to the Seminole to encourage a unified Native American front against white encroachment, specifically that of the Americans.

The Seminole, perhaps more than any of the Five Civilized Tribes, rejected the notion of giving up their land and being moved west of the Mississippi. The nativist leaders among the Creek were Josiah Francis, Peter McQueen, High Head Jim, and Paddy Walsh. They opposed leaders like Big Warrior, who interacted with US Indian Agent Benjamin Hawkins and supported the construction of roads through Creek territory without consent from other tribal leaders.

Civil war broke out in the Creek Confederation during the War of 1812. The nativists, now called Red Sticks, were attacked by United States forces while crossing Burnt Corn Creek in Alabama after receiving ammunition from the British in Florida territory. In response, they attacked the settlement of Samuel Mims. The Fort Mims Massacre occurred on August 30th, 1813, when a group of Red Sticks led by Peter McQueen and Red Eagle attacked and captured the fort, which was poorly defended and commanded by Major Daniel Beasley, who disregarded reports of Native Americans in the area and was known to be drunk while on duty. The Red Sticks burned the fort and killed an estimated 500 people, including soldiers, slaves, mixed-blood Creeks, and white settlers, including women and children. Most of the slaves were not killed but captured. Only thirty-six people managed to escape, mostly men. The Red Sticks then killed most of the livestock and destroyed the fields of the settlement. It is believed about 100 Red Sticks died in the fight.

This turned the civil war among the Creek into a war between the Creek and the US. Georgie, Tennessee, and Mississippi territory organized their militia, led by Major General Andrew Jackson. The conflict eventually ended at the Battle of Horseshoe Bend in modern-day Alabama with a US victory and the end of the Red Sticks, many of whom fled south into Florida. The general then negotiated the Treaty of Fort

Jackson, which ended with the Creek, both friend and foe, losing twenty million acres.

In Florida, the British had been arming Seminole, Miccosukee, and runaway enslaved people for some time. With the end of the War of 1812, the Red Sticks that had fled to Florida were quick to affirm their alliance with the British; they even donned British uniforms and could be seen walking the streets of Pensacola. When Jackson heard of this, he petitioned the US government to let him take Pensacola, which was near his stunning victory at New Orleans and very close to the US port city of Mobile.

Native Americans and escaped slaves were supported by the British army, which could not afford another direct conflict with the US. They established a fort at Prospect Bluff and were given food by John Forbes & Company, who owned a large portion of the Florida panhandle thanks to debt owed by Creek and Seminole traders. The US Army called the spot on Prospect Bluff the Negro Fort because it was manned exclusively by former slaves and Native Americans. Though Spain officially owned Florida, it did not have the capacity to help or stop the actions of the Seminole, former slaves, or the British. The Spanish lodged complaints, but those fell on deaf ears. The number of Native American and formerly enslaved fighters at Prospect Bluff outnumbered the number of Spanish soldiers in West and East Florida.

Jackson received the blessing of the US government and proceeded to begin maneuvers against the Seminole and Black forces at Prospect Bluff. After various skirmishes, gunboats arrived and hit a magazine within the fort, causing a massive explosion. Of the 300 people inside the fort, including women and children, 270 were killed by the explosion. The American soldiers captured almost all remaining people in the fort; they gave free slaves back to Spanish and Native American owners and tortured the rest until they died. Everyone living near Pensacola fled into the interior of Florida, many joining with the Seminole that were already there. The border between Spanish Florida and the US states of Georgia and Alabama became areas of increased tension as many Americans began to engage in raids to the south to find escaped slaves or capture cattle, while Native Americans also raided to the north to stop the incursion of whites into their land.

Jackson ordered a new fort to be built on the Flint River, close to the border with Florida. Across from the site of the fort was a Miccosukee village named Fowltown, which was run by a miko named Neamathla. Under the command of General Gaines, men from the fort entered a forest near the village to obtain lumber. Neamathla told Gaines he would not allow such trespasses. Gaines informed Neamathla that the land in question had been ceded by the Treaty of Fort Jackson, as was the land that Fowltown sat on, so Neamathla and his people were subject to US law. Neamathla replied that he had signed no such treaty and that the land was theirs. Of course, both men, from their point of view, were correct. The land of Fowltown was part of the treaty, but Neamathla did not consider himself subject to the treaty. The land, like everything else, was communally owned and used by his people. They had not given it over to the United States. They could use the forest, but the troops would need to ask before cutting down trees.

As a result of this impasse, open conflict erupted in November of 1817. This was the beginning of the First Seminole War. The Americans attacked Fowltown, and the Seminole, along with free Africans, escaped slaves, and others of African descent known as Black Seminoles, retaliated by attacking a boat filled with reinforcements on the Apalachicola River, killing forty-three.

General Jackson was then given command of forces in the south and invaded Florida, destroying Seminole towns as he went. He took Pensacola and captured the Spanish military post at St. Marks. These actions helped lead to Spain ceding Florida to the US. In exchange, the US would not challenge Spain's control of Texas. The Seminole eventually agreed to a surrender in which they were removed to a reservation in central Florida and forced to give up their lands in northern Florida under the Treaty of Moultrie Creek.

The US nullified this treaty when it demanded that the Seminoles relocate to Oklahoma as part of the Indian Removal Act. The Seminole fought back, using guerilla tactics to successfully frustrate the US Army's efforts to destroy them. This would be the Second Seminole War, which lasted from 1835 to 1842. It finally ended when General Thomas Jesup gained command of the forces in Florida and began to destroy Seminole farms, towns, and homes to starve them out. He then treasonously kidnapped two Seminole leaders, Osceola and Micanopy, under a false flag of truce. There was no official peace treaty, though many Seminole did relocate to Oklahoma.

A Third Seminole War erupted in 1855 when settlers began to clash with Seminole in southern Florida. The Americans again responded by destroying ranches and farms. By 1858, many more Seminole agreed to relocate. Bands of only about 100 to 300 Seminole remained in Florida, moving into the Everglades and Big Cypress Swamp, land that was deemed unsuitable for white settlers.

From these few, every Seminole currently living in Florida—about 2,000 in total—is descended. They call themselves the "Unconquered People," truly a fitting sobriquet. Instead of the animal hides and crafts of their ancestors, modern-day Seminole in Florida grow citrus fruit and raise cattle. Tourism and bingo profits pay for schools on their reservations, established after the Seminole Tribe of Florida gained federal recognition in the 1950s. In 1970, the Seminole in Oklahoma and Florida were awarded over $12 million for the land they had lost to the US military. Today, some still live in the thatch-roofed open-air structures called *chickees.*

Chapter 5: Muscogee Creek

The Muscogee (also spelled Muskogee) were known and are still often known as the Creek, a name the British gave to a much larger population of Native Americans. Like the Choctaw and Cherokee, the Muscogee descended from the Mississippian culture. They lived in modern-day Alabama and southern Georgia, and from them came the Seminole people.

Like the other Five Civilized Tribes, the Muscogee were separated into clans, which acted as extended families, and also into towns led by councils and chiefs. After being decimated by disease and conflict with neighboring tribes, the Muscogee consolidated and moved into the interior and away from the coasts. They were often at odds with the Cherokee, and the British used this to their benefit by encouraging raids and warfare between the two tribes. They supplied the Muscogee with firearms, cloth, and metal tools in exchange for furs, crops, and slaves.

After the creation of the United States of America, the Creek found themselves in the middle of hotly contested territory: the modern-day states of Mississippi, Alabama, and Louisiana, and western Florida, also called the "panhandle." This Old Southwest was home to the Creek, but the Americans, Spanish, and British all had claims to it. The most aggressive claimant was also the most recent—the United States. Americans were continually pushing the boundaries and attempting to settle in land previously excluded from them via treaty. Their way of life, plantation farming, required large expanses of land to produce vast amounts of cash crops processed by slave labor. The Americans wanted land, and the

Creek had it. The Spanish seemed most interested in keeping what was theirs—that is, the territory of Florida, which at the time also included the area around the port of Mobile. The Spanish had a new ally in the British, their one-time enemy, who wanted back what they had lost in the American Revolution. This situation became particularly volatile in the early 19th century and would lead to two overlapping wars: the War of 1812 and the Creek War.

The American settlers in Georgia and Mississippi Territory were concerned that the new British-Spanish alliance would arm Native Americans and instigate them into attacking settlements. The British had already done this in the Northwest Territory north of the Ohio River. In fact, the British would arm the Creek in Florida. There was a concern that this activity could also be the preliminary tactic to a British invasion from the Gulf of Mexico. These concerns helped push America closer to war with Britain, along with the fact that the British did not abandon forts as they said they would in the Treaty of Paris. The British were also pressing American sailors into service in the Royal Navy.

The Creek were divided on how they viewed the increasing encroachment by Americans. By the 19th century, many of the Creek had been marrying Americans and British settlers, so there was a large group of Creek that were as much of European descent as Native American. The Upper Creek began to grow tired of the Americans' attempts to change their way of life and destroy their traditions. However, the Lower Creek felt differently. From their point of view, the best option was to make peace with the Americans.

In 1811, Tecumseh traveled to Creek territory and preached his message against the Americans. He believed that the only way to ensure the survival of the Native Americans was to form a great confederacy against the United States. His vision became a religious crusade thanks in part to Tecumseh's brother, Tenskwatawa, or "The Prophet." The appearance of a comet in the sky and the New Madrid earthquake of 1812 seemed to support Tecumseh's prophetic warnings. While he was largely unsuccessful with the Choctaw, Chickasaw, and many of the Creek, some of the Upper Creek joined together in a call for a return to traditional ways and an active resistance against the Americans. That group of Muscogee would be known as the Red Sticks after the particular color of their wooden war clubs.

The Red Sticks were soon at war with the rest of the Creek, sometimes called the White Sticks for their preference for peace with the Americans. Violence between the Red Sticks and American settlers was not far behind. The Red Sticks would attack settlers, killing men, women, and children. The federal agent Hawkins would work with the White Sticks to find the Creek responsible, who would be handed over to the Americans and executed. This series of events would repeat again and again throughout 1812 and into 1813.

What erupted in July of 1813 would be called the Creek War. It would pit the Red Sticks, with material support from the British and Spanish, against the White Sticks and American militia from Georgia, Tennessee, and Mississippi Territory. The Red Sticks attacked Tuckabatchee, a mother town of the Muscogee Creek Confederation. The White Sticks replied by burning many Red Stick towns. A group of Red Sticks were attacked by American militia on July 27th, 1813. The Red Sticks were returning from Pensacola and fled, but regrouped and attacked the looting Americans and won the Battle of Burnt Corn. The attack on Fort Mims was carried out a month later. Colonel Andrew Jackson was called out to lead a militia of 2,500 men from west Tennessee to join with an equal force from east Tennessee to stop the Creek in Mississippi Territory. Several White Stick Creek and the Cherokee joined the army to stop the Red Sticks.

The Georgia Militia of 1,500 men, including friendly Creek, advanced into Mississippi Territory and was met by a Red Stick army of 1,300—the largest force they would raise in the war. The Georgians repulsed the Red Stick attack but retreated to Fort Mitchell after the Battle of Calebee Creek. The Mississippi Militia reached the Holy Ground, the center of Red Sticks' territory. They did not engage in battle but burned down some 260 homes. Andrew Jackson's force set out from Tennessee by October 1813. His mission was to stop the Red Sticks, but his larger aim was to attack Pensacola, which was under Spanish control. On November 3rd, part of Jackson's cavalry defeated Red Stick forces in the Battle of Tallushatchee; they then defeated more Red Sticks at the Battle of Talladega.

After months of issues with supply shortages, the dismissal of several troops, and the desertion of additional forces combined with the delay in receiving reinforcements, Jackson could not take to the field again until March of 1814. The Red Sticks had a force of roughly 1,000 warriors.

Jackson commanded about 3,300 fighters, including allied Native Americans, and also had artillery. They met at the Battle of Horseshoe Bend in modern-day Alabama, where Jackson's army attacked the Red Sticks in a log and dirt fortification of their own construction. Jackson hit them with cannon fire and ordered a charge up the hill to the fort. One of the first over the wall was Sam Houston, the future leader of Texas, who was struck by a Creek arrow. The Red Sticks were surrounded but refused to surrender. Of the 1,000 warriors present, almost all of them were killed in the battle. Two hundred Creek were able to escape and joined the Seminole in Florida.

This would mark the end of the Creek War. The Muscogee Creek had to sign the Treaty of Fort Jackson on August 9th, 1814. The treaty required the Creek, Red and White alike, to surrender twenty-three million acres of land.

After the Treaty of Fort Jackson, Tennessee used the Creek War as an excuse to demand the removal of the Cherokee, Creek, and Chickasaw. Georgia had been able to remove the Creek from the state in the Treaty of Fort Jackson, and Alabama hoped to do the same by extending its laws over all Native American lands and refusing to recognize the sovereignty of several Creek settlements. Creek who claimed allotments for private ownership were subject to harassment by their white neighbors. From 1820 to 1840, the Muscogee Creek were systematically forced to leave the southeastern United States and go to the Indian Territory that would become Oklahoma—another Trail of Tears. Still, some remained in Alabama and etched out a meager existence. Those who traveled west were in no better position. They refused aid that had been promised to them by the federal government and focused on rebuilding their nation. During the American Civil War, the Muscogee split into two factions, one that supported the Union and the other that supported the Confederacy. These factions fought each other, and the pro-Union side left for Kansas until after the war.

The Muscogee (Creek) formed a new government, selected a capital at Okmulgee, Oklahoma, and built a capital building in 1866 and 1867. The end of the 19th century was a prosperous time for the nation, as it had little interference from the federal government. The 1898 Curtis Act, however, dismantled Native American governments in another attempt to assimilate Native Americans into white society. The Dawes Allotment Act required tribes to break up their communal holdings into private allotments. This led the way for Oklahoma to become a state in 1907. As a result of the Dawes Act, the Muscogee, along with many other tribes, lost large amounts of land deemed "surplus" by the federal government and sold privately. The federal government also separated the Muscogee population into three categories: "Creek by blood," Creek Freedmen," and "Intermarried Whites." The process was so hastily done that members of the same family, especially in the case of Freedmen (descendants of freed slaves), were placed in separate groups regardless of their true status. The Muscogee (Creek) did not reorganize and regain federal status until 1970.

Chapter 6: Other Tribes

The Shawnee

The Shawnee are an Algonquian-speaking people who lived in southern Ohio, West Virginia, and western Pennsylvania. In the 1660s, they were driven from this land by the Haudenosaunee, or Iroquois, to take these rich hunting grounds. For a time, they remained scattered, but by 1730, many had returned to the Ohio River Valley. They joined with other tribes to resist the British in 1761. This uprising was stopped; however, they joined Ottawa Chief Pontiac in his resistance to the British just two years later. They were stopped again. During Lord Dunmore's War of 1774, they fought against the Virginians. Due to the Virginian victory at the Battle of Point Pleasant, the Shawnee were forced to give up all their land south of the Ohio River. The tribe scattered again. One group settled in Missouri and became known as the Absentee Shawnee.

Shawnee chiefs Blue Jacket, Little Turtle, and most famously, Tecumseh fought against American incursion into what was then called the Northwest Territory but would one day be the present states of Ohio, Indiana, Illinois, Michigan, and Wisconsin. Tecumseh brought together many tribes from all over the American frontier to face the Americans at the same time the US declared war on Britain in the War of 1812. Tecumseh sided with the British and led several successful battles against the Americans, but the British were never willing to offer anything greater than material and token support. So, American generals Anthony Wayne and William Henry Harrison and their allies defeated the Shawnee. Many of the Shawnees were wiped out, and those that remained moved west of the Mississippi. During the Civil War, those that sided with the Union called themselves Loyal Shawnee. In 1869, they moved to land offered to them by the Cherokee. They became federally recognized in 2000.

The Pawnee

The Pawnee lived along the tributaries of the Missouri River in what would be Kansas and central Nebraska. When the Europeans made first contact with the Pawnee, the tribe numbered tens of thousands and was one of the largest on the plains. The Pawnee are separated into four bands: the Skiri, the Chaui (Chawis), the Kitkahahki, and the Pitahawirata, each occupying a village. The Pawnee lived in a semi-sedentary yearly cycle. In the spring, they dwelt in earth lodges with domed roofs that housed up to twenty people. During this season, women planted and tended gardens of corn, bean, and squash. Men were occupied with religious rituals. In June, the Pawnee would travel west into the High Plains. There they lived in temporary bowl-shaped shelters and hunted bison for three months. In late August, they would return to harvest their gardens and engage in ritual activities. Then in October and November, they traveled west again to partake in the winter bison hunt. During this time, they lived in bison hide tipis. In February or March, they would return to their earth lodges to wait for the coming of spring.

Like many Native American tribes, Pawnee life was centered around the village. However, over time, the number of villages varied, as did the population of each village. At times, villages could consist of several thousand people, and there could be hundreds of villages at any given time. When Europeans first made contact with the Pawnee, they noted that the villages were large but few in number, while various bands might coincide with a village, or a village might be made up of several bands. Each band or village was led by four chiefs—a head chief and three subordinate chiefs. The position of chief was hereditary, though someone could gain the position through merit, mainly success in war. Each village had a sacred bundle, a religious shrine representing the history of that particular village or band. The head chief owned the bundle, and his wife cared for it, but a head priest knew the rituals and religious ceremonies associated with it. The chief also had young attendants who lived with him, known simply as "boys." The Pawnee had both priests and doctors. The priests were largely concerned with the welfare of the village and bringing good fortune to the community. Their gods were the gods of the heavens. Doctors, on the other hand, focused on the curative properties of animals and plants. Animals, including insects, might bless people in dreams, for instance. These animals could bestow powers on individuals.

The expansionist United States first began to impact the Pawnee in the 19th century when wagons and railroad lines began to cut across their territory. Then whites began to inhabit parts of Pawnee land. As emigration increased, things that had once been plentiful were now becoming scarce, such as bison, wood, and pastures. It was not only whites who moved into Pawnee land but also displaced tribes from east of the Mississippi that had been forcibly removed from their lands and given Pawnee land by the United States. In 1833, the Pawnee were forced to give up their land south of the Platte River. In 1857, they were confined to a small reservation on the Platte River. The Pawnee also suffered a series of epidemics that tore through their population. Throughout much of their history, they were at war with the Sioux and were in almost continual conflict with most of the other tribes of the Great Plains. However, in 1833, they renounced warfare completely and gave up their weapons. The Sioux then began a campaign of extermination against the now-helpless Pawnee, who were not protected by the federal government.

In the Indian Wars after the American Civil War, Pawnee often acted as scouts for the US Army as they fought the Sioux, Cheyenne, and Arapaho. They also served as protectors for workers constructing the transcontinental railroad. In 1874, the Pawnee gave up their reservation in Nebraska and moved to Indian Territory in Oklahoma on Cherokee land. Today, this is the majority of what makes up Pawnee County. At first, the Pawnee continued their traditional way of life in which separate bands lived in villages and farmland was collectively owned and farmed by the villagers. They were led by chiefs, priests, and doctors. However, by the turn of the century, many Pawnees had begun living on privately-owned farms, dressing like whites, and speaking English. They no longer hunted bison but instead bred livestock and cash crops. The sacred bundles, priests, and doctors began to vanish. Chiefs were replaced with agents. It was determined that only one-third of the reservation could be cultivated, and the yield was low. Livestock also had difficulty surviving in these conditions. The sanitation on the reservation was poor, and the Pawnee's health suffered even more. By 1901, their population reached an all-time low of 629, and it did not grow until the 1930s.

In 1936, the Pawnee established a tribal constitution with a chief's council and a business council. By the 1960s, they had regained lost land outside the town of Pawnee. They also acquired the building complex of the Pawnee Indian School. In 1980, they built a tribal roundhouse based on the earth lodges of their past. Today, the Pawnee Nation owns administrative buildings, a nursing home, a hospital, a gymnasium, a smoke shop, and a truck stop on the reservation. Every four years, they hold a homecoming in which Pawnee from around the world come back to the reservation to participate in community dances and visit with relatives.

The Sioux

The name "Sioux" is short for Nadouessioux, which means "enemy" in the language of the Ojibwa people. The Sioux include a very large range of people who speak three different Siouan languages. The Santee or Eastern Sioux were Dakota speakers, the Yankton spoke Nakota, and the Teton or Western Sioux spoke Lakota. Each of these groups was made up of different tribes. In the 17th century, the Santee lived along Lake Superior, gathering wild rice and hunting deer and bison. Due to constant war with the Ojibwa, the Santee moved into modern-day Minnesota, thus pushing the Yankton and Teton into North and South Dakota. These groups had been largely agricultural, but due to the appearance of horses from European expeditions, they began to focus more on hunting bison and developed a more nomadic lifestyle.

The Teton and Yankton shared similarities with tribes of the Great Plains. They lived in tipis, wore leather clothes, and traded buffalo products for other types of food. All of the Sioux tribes were highly religious and believed in four powers that presided over the universe. They used shamanism to deal with supernatural forces. Most men focused on hunting and warfare, raiding neighboring tribes like the Pawnee. Women processed buffalo hides, which were used by the tribe or traded for goods. The most important yearly event was the Sun Dance.

In the 19th century, the United States began encroaching on Sioux territory, which included Montana, Wyoming, Colorado, Nebraska, and North and South Dakota. In 1851, the Sioux signed the Treaty of Fort Laramie. The treaty caused the Santee to give up their territory in Minnesota and settle on a reservation in exchange for annuities. However, the annuities were mismanaged. A lack of game and resistance to an agrarian lifestyle led to starvation on the reservation by 1862. In that year, the Santee attempted to reclaim their territory. The US Army was called in to stop what would be called the Sioux Uprising. Four hundred settlers, seventy US soldiers, and thirty Santee died in the conflict, while several Santee were sentenced to death for their part in the resistance. President Lincoln commuted many of the sentences, but thirty-eight men were hung in the largest mass execution in United States history.

In 1866, Chief High Backbone led a campaign in which he drew a US military patrol of eighty men into an ambush where all the Americans were killed. Among the Sioux involved in the Fetterman Massacre was Crazy Horse. The US government, recognizing the futility of developing the Plains, gave the Sioux all of South Dakota west of the Missouri River in the Second Treaty of Fort Laramie in 1868. However, when gold was discovered in the Black Hills, American prospectors ignored the treaty and flooded into the territory. The Sioux's greatest victory was also the beginning of their defeat when 200 soldiers under the command of Lt. Col. George Custer were killed in the Battle of the Little Bighorn. The response was known as the Plains Wars, and it ended in 1876 when the tribes formally surrendered and most returned to their reservations.

However, Sitting Bull, Crazy Horse, and Chief Gall refused to return to the reservations. Crazy Horse eventually surrendered but was killed for resisting arrest for leaving his reservation. He was reportedly taking his ill wife to see relatives. Chiefs Sitting Bull and Gall entered Canada and remained there for several years but returned and surrendered without incident. By the end of the 19th century, the Ghost Dance religion came to the Sioux people and promised the coming of a messiah and the disappearance of all European descendants from North America. Sitting Bull was ordered by the US not to attend Ghost Dance meetings. When he disobeyed this order in 1890, he was killed. In the same year, the US 7th Cavalry, Custer's old regiment, killed 200 men, women, and children at Wounded Knee Creek. The Sioux then ceased resisting the US military, with many of them serving in that military over the years. In 1973, some Sioux activists symbolically took control of Wounded Knee in what is known as the Wounded Knee Occupation.

Today there are roughly 160,000 Sioux people in the United States.

The Navajo

It is believed that, from 900 to 1250 BCE, the Navajo people of Northwest New Mexico developed a rich and complex culture with a vast trade network between the Anasazi people and the Pueblo people. In the sixteenth century, they had contact with the Spanish. In 1680, they joined the Pueblo and Apache in the Pueblo Revolt against Spain, forcing the

Spanish into Mexico for a time. But, in 1693, the Spanish returned and reconquered the Rio Grande Valley. Many Pueblo sought refuge with the Navajo, and this created a blended society with elements of both groups intertwined. The Navajo quickly adopted the use of horses, which they sometimes stole from the Spanish. They also raised sheep and goats, which the Spanish introduced to the area. By the eighteenth century, they had moved into southern Utah and northern Arizona. The Spanish allied themselves with Comanche and Ute groups and conquered the entire southwest, enslaving many Navajo.

By the late nineteenth century, the Navajo were mainly fighting against American forces. Under Christopher "Kit" Carson, the US used scorched-earth tactics to eventually force the Navajo to surrender. After 1863, the Navajo were forced to conduct what would be known as the Long Walk, a forced march from their homeland to central New Mexico. Many died on the journey, but those who survived were confined to the small, crowded, and unsanitary Bosque Redondo Reservation at Fort Sumner. However, in 1868, a new treaty was signed that allowed them to return to their homeland. The Navajo Reservation, today known as the Navajo Nation, would eventually cover 27,000 square miles in Arizona, Utah, and New Mexico.

For the Navajo themselves, their origin is a much different story, typically referred to as the Story of the Emergence. In this story, First Man and First Woman, along with their people, emerged from the First World to the Fourth World, also known as the Earth-Surface World. The First Man brought four sacred mountains with him from the Third World, marking the sacred homeland land of the Navajo people. Today, the mountains are known as Blanca Peak in Colorado, Mount Taylor in New Mexico, Mount Humphreys in Arizona, and Hesperus Peak in Colorado. To the Navajo, however, they are the White Mountain, the Turquoise Mountain, the Yellow Mountain, and the Dark Mountain, respectively.

The Navajo gained prominence during World War II when their language was used to deceive the Japanese. The "Code Talkers" were Navajo men of exceptional bravery who became heroes in the Pacific Theater, but they were not alone. Thousands of Navajos joined the Army, Navy, Marine Corps, and Women's Army Corps, not to mention those who left the reservation to work in war-related industries. Today, the population of the Navajo Nation is over 250,000. The Navajo government consists of executive, legislative, and judicial branches, and the Navajo

Nation Council consists of 88 delegates representing 110 Navajo Nation Chapters. It is one of the most successful Native American government bodies in existence.

The Comanche

The Comanche call themselves Nermernuh. The name "Comanche" is a Ute word that means "anyone who wants to fight me all the time." The Comanche were originally part of the Wyoming Shoshone but broke apart and moved south, displacing other tribes such as the Apache. They spoke an Uto-Aztecan language, which is among North America's largest and oldest language families, with speakers at one time stretching from Oregon to Panama. By the nineteenth century, they were a large and powerful tribe consisting of anywhere from 7,000 to 30,000 people.

Like other Native Americans of the Great Plains, the Comanche quickly adopted the use of horses from the Spanish. They lived a largely nomadic lifestyle, following and hunting bison herds. Their main industry was processing bison into coats, tipi coverings, water holders, and items sold or traded for other goods. By the end of the 19th century, there were thirteen distinct bands within the tribe, the main five being the Yamparika (Yap Eaters), Kotsoteka (Bison Eaters), Penateka (Honey Eaters), Nokoni (Wanderers, or Those Who Turn Back), and the Quahadis (Antelopes).

In 1864, Kit Carson led an unsuccessful campaign against the Comanche. The following year, the Comanche signed a treaty with the US in which they were promised western Oklahoma; however, the U.S government did little to keep squatters from entering their territory. In 1867, tension increased between the Comanche and the US, resulting in violence. Following this, the Comanche were to be settled on a reservation in Oklahoma, but white squatters continued to encroach on their land. Fighting continued between the two. Still, not all the Comanche bands settled on the reservation. Quanah Parker led the Antelope Comanche during the Red River War, which ended in 1875 when Parker and his Comanche band surrendered to the US Army at Fort Sill and settled on the Comanche reservation in Oklahoma.

Attempts to turn the Comanche into farmers were generally unsuccessful, but they did raise livestock. In 1930, the discovery of oil and natural gas along the Red River benefited some tribes when they leased their allotments to oil companies. Some landowners became very wealthy in the 1970s and 1980s from this arrangement. A casino was also opened at the tribal capital of Lawton, and the proceeds go towards important tribal initiatives. Today, the Comanche number in the tens of thousands.

The Apache

The name "Apache" is a generalized one. Various groups under that umbrella term have also been called Yutaglen-ne, Ypandi, Tontos, Querechos, Natagee, Gilenos, Faraones, Mescalero, Lipan, and Apachu, among others. The name Apachu was used by the Onate people to describe a group living in the southern plains. The Spanish changed the name to Apache and used it to describe various groups, but it was not used universally until the nineteenth century. The people then referred to as Apache had roots in Canada and the areas of the Northern Great Plains. They eventually migrated south and lived in the Southern Plains of Texas, Oklahoma, and New Mexico. When Coronado traveled along the Southern Plains in 1541, he met the Querechos and Teya people, who were most likely Apache.

It is not known exactly when the Apache migrated south, but when they did, they separated into two distinct groups—the Eastern Apache and Western Apache. There were other subdivisions beyond that. Like most Native Americans, the main societal unit was the extended family, which could be quite large and was often called a village by European explorers and American settlers. Large groups, sometimes called bands, often existed, as well as even larger groups, often identified as tribes. However, this distinction is always from a European or American perspective and is often not how the people saw themselves. The Spanish used the terms Navajo and Apache interchangeably, but today they are seen as very separate groups. Some of the divisions of the Apache are identified by name, such as the Mescalero Apache and Lipan. Other group names, like the Pelones, did not become preeminent in identification by outsiders.

The Apache eventually moved even farther south as the Comanche migrated into their territory. Eventually, in the 18th century, they settled along the Pecos River and the Rio Grande, where they worried the Spanish, who saw them as a threat. The Apache, however, were more concerned with the westward movement of the British and then the Americans. They allied with their previous enemies, the Jumano and Tonkawa, and allowed the Spanish to establish missions within their territory. One mission, the Santa Cruz de San Sabá, also had a fort, or *presidio*. This was eventually attacked by the Comanche and other allies, all enemies of the Apache, and was abandoned. The missions were not particularly successful, as they wanted to convince the Apache to give up their nomadic lifestyle and grow crops like corn. The Apache range was far and wide, and raids and hunting trips were conducted into Mexico and across the Great Plains. When America went to war with Mexico in 1846, the Apache gave the US safe passage through their lands and recognized America's claims over previous portions of Mexico. However, in the 1850s, violence broke out between the Americans and the Apache in what is sometimes called "The Apache Wars." In 1875, America forcefully removed 1,500 Apache from their homeland to march 180 miles to the Indian Agency in San Carlos. Still, other Apache resisted. The final defeat came in 1886 when Geronimo's band of fifty men, women, and children were forced to surrender to 5,000 American soldiers in Arizona.

The Mescalero Apache Reservation was created by executive order on May 27, 1873, by President Ulysses S. Grant. At first, the Apache there only numbered 400, but others have joined them over the years. They formed a government run by a Tribal Council of eight members, with a President and Vice-president. Their constitution was established in 1965.

SECTION TWO:
TRAILS AND TRIBULATIONS

Chapter 7: Andrew Jackson and Martin Van Buren

Andrew Jackson, seventh president of the United States of America.
https://commons.wikimedia.org/wiki/File:Andrew_jackson_head.jpg

Born to Irish immigrants in the Carolina backcountry, Andrew Jackson certainly came from humble beginnings. His father, the senior Andrew Jackson, died before young Jackson was even born. His birth was in 1767 in the Waxhaws region of the Carolina colony; there is still some debate about whether he was born in North or South Carolina. The American Revolution began when he was just a teenager, but he joined his older brothers and became a boy soldier, intending to fight the oppressive British and gain American independence. His brother Hugh died of exposure while he was away fighting. Andrew and his other brother, Robert, were captured and contracted smallpox. The disease killed Robert but left Andrew, who had never been a particularly healthy child, devastated by the illness. His mother managed to get Jackson released and brought him home, but she suddenly died of cholera not long after. Jackson was left without a family and had to rely on the kindness of his neighbors in Waxhaws. Despite his trials, he grew into a hard-drinking, gambling rake fond of horses and prone to dueling. He held his honor in the highest regard and did not tolerate any blemish in himself or those he cared for.

After the formation of the United States, Jackson studied the law and gained employment in Nashville, Tennessee, which was then a frontier town. There he met and married Rachel Donelson, who had been attacked by Native Americans as a child on her way to live in Tennessee. Rachel had been married before but was divorced. This never concerned Jackson but would cause issues for him later in life. He entered politics in 1795 as a staunch Jeffersonian, opposed to a strong central government. He was popular due to his origins: voters felt he could relate to their hardscrabble life. He became a US Senator and built a large plantation called the Hermitage, where he owned many slaves and grew cotton. He quickly became one of the wealthiest men in Tennessee.

Jackson, as a citizen and representative of frontiersmen, always viewed Native Americans as an enemy, specifically any Native Americans that would not submit to American power. In 1802, he became a major general of the State Militia of Tennessee. At the onset of the War of 1812, Jackson was anxious to play a part in the fight. When he received orders in 1813 to contain the Native American threat in Florida and Southern Alabama, he must have relished the opportunity, and he proved equal to the challenge.

Jackson and his men were especially motivated after the Massacre at Fort Mims; Jackson is said to have been particularly outraged by these events. However, as is often the case, things were more complicated than they might first appear. Jackson did not believe, for instance, that all Native Americans were essentially evil, and he did not, despite what some contend, believe Native Americans should be exterminated. Samuel Mims himself was part Native American, as were many of the men in the militia, and many of Jackson's allies were Cherokee. In one battle, a Cherokee saved Jackson's life. However, Jackson most certainly felt that Native Americans were of an inferior race to his own and that they should thus submit to American control. If a Native American killed a white settler, that Native American's life was forfeited, as far as Jackson was concerned. After overseeing the slaughter at Tallushatchee, Jackson reported happily to his superiors that he had killed 200 Native Americans. As one of the soldiers, Davy Crockett, put it, they had "shot them like dogs."

Jackson's militia and the allied Creek and Cherokee eventually overwhelmed the Red Sticks at Horseshoe Bend, thus completing and perhaps going beyond Jackson's mission to contain the threat. Jackson was awarded a position as a major general in the regular army for his work. Between 1816 and 1820, he signed five treaties with Native Americans to gain tens of millions of acres from enemies and allies alike. In 1817, Jackson experimented with forced removal in a treaty secured with bribes from the Cherokee. He exchanged two million acres in Tennessee, Georgia, and Alabama for two million in Arkansas. Jackson was an expansionist and believed that the United States needed more land for its growing population and agricultural industry. Native Americans were in the way of his idea of progress. With that in mind, he also took the fight into Spanish Florida in the First Seminole War, eventually gaining Florida as a new state.

Jackson ran for president in 1824 but narrowly lost to John Quincy Adams. He ran again in four years and won the position of Commander and Chief. His success at the poles was a statement on the changing nature of American politics at the time. Jackson was not a member of the southern aristocracy or the northern intellectual elite; he was a commoner. However, he was far from common in his ambitions, principles, and successes. He was one of the first American "rags to riches" stories and the preeminent military hero of his age. As president, he had much that he wanted to accomplish. He desired to end the Second Bank of the United States, which he thought was too powerful, and to move to hard currency. He was concerned with the growing animosity between anti-slavery protesters and slave owners, including himself. In his first inaugural address, he promised to observe a "just and liberal" policy towards Native Americans. It was the promise of a politician—vague and elusive, promising nothing.

In 1829, Georgia wanted to remove the Cherokees from their state, partly because of the discovery of gold on Cherokee land. Jackson felt it was time to establish a clear federal policy on all Native American issues and believed the best policy for the US was the "voluntary" relocation of all Native Americans to areas west of the Mississippi. In this spirit, he put forward the Indian Removal Act. This proposed law would manage the migration of thousands of Native Americans. Several people wrote in protest of Jackson's treatment of Native Americans, but Jackson believed the protests were organized by his political enemies and not true expressions of a desire for Native American rights. The Cherokee argued that they were a sovereign state and a separate nation, but Jackson disagreed. He did not believe having separate nations inside US territory was constitutional. Jackson made sure pro-removal people were in key positions, and Jackson's protégé, Martin Van Buren, worked tirelessly to secure the vote to make Indian removal the law, even though he wondered if it might damage him politically. When the Indian Removal Act narrowly passed in 1830, Jackson couldn't have been more pleased. He felt the best thing for Americans and Native Americans was removal under federal protection so that Native Americans could live as they wanted. Indian removal was not genocidal, but in its application, it had no respect for Native American life.

Removal turned out to be ruinous for Native Americans—not the paternal protection Jackson and others had sold to Native Americans and the US population. The allotment schemes in which Native Americans could receive private property led to fraud in which swindlers bought land from Native Americans for much less than it was worth. This left many homeless and caused them to turn to criminal actions. This was true of the Creek in Alabama and led to 15,000 being forced west. Insufficient funds were provided for the journey, which led to horrible conditions on the "Trail of Tears." Thousands died of smallpox, cholera, malnutrition, and exposure. It was perhaps the first death march in recorded history.

The Cherokee fought back in the courts. In the Supreme Court case *Cherokee v. Georgia*, the court ruled that the Cherokee were a domestic dependent state. Things were clarified in *Worcester v. Georgia*, in which the court dictated that the state of Georgia did not have authority over the Cherokee, who were only under federal jurisdiction. This was problematic for Jackson because he relied on state authorities to make things unfavorable to Native Americans and thus convince them to "volunteer" for removal. However, Georgia refused to recognize the court's ruling, and Jackson refused to enforce it.

Jackson is rightfully remembered as an enemy to all Native Americans, even those he counted as allies, because his insistence on the "solution" of removal was based on racist ideas and was at the very least patronizing to Native Americans and at the worst very deadly. By 1837, Jackson's administration had removed 46,000 Native Americans from their homelands into lands west of the Mississippi River, many of them at the point of a bayonet. Native Americans were often not allowed to collect their belongings, and whites would ransack their homes as they left.

While much of Indian removal was enforced by Jackson, more was left to his handpicked predecessor, Martin Van Buren. Van Buren, like Jackson, had come from humble beginnings, but their starting points were many miles apart. Van Buren had been the son of a tavern keeper in Kinderhook, New York. Also, like Jackson, he was a lawyer who had first raised himself through state politics and then was elected to the US Senate. He became the most famous northern Jacksonian and was appointed Secretary of State by Jackson. Van Buren soon showed himself to be Jackson's trusted advisor within the Cabinet. After Vice-President John C. Calhoun and Jackson quarreled, Jackson made Van Buren his new vice-president in his second term. Van Buren gained the nickname the "Little Magician" for his short stature and ability to negotiate tough political circumstances. Van Buren then became the 8th President of the United States thanks largely to Jackson's support.

When Van Buren took office, thousands of Native Americans had already been relocated as part of the Indian Removal Act of 1830. Van Buren supported the act completely and intended to enforce it with as much vigor as his mentor. Van Buren saw his role as a guardian and benefactor to Native Americans. How he rectified this image with reports of thousands dying on the Trail of Tears is unknown. His main goal as a "benefactor" was to round up the last of the Cherokee east of the Mississippi and force them to move to land in the west. A group of Cherokee had signed the Treaty of New Echota, which relinquished all Cherokee land east of the Mississippi, but the signers did not represent the entire Cherokee population. Van Buren disregarded this and sent the army to capture the Cherokee and put them in internment camps.

These remaining Cherokee were then forced to walk the Trail of Tears, with an estimated 4,000 dying during the winter march of 1838. For Van Buren, however, it had been a success—one of the few of his tarnished one-term in office. Not long after taking office, the country was hit by the Panic of 1837, the worst financial crisis in its history. Van Buren's economic policies proved ineffective with the problem, and he lost his bid for a second term. His efforts to stop the annexation of Texas also proved insufficient, as the state entered the union not long after he left office. His fear of war with Mexico was realized. He ran for the presidency again on the Free Soil ticket, as he was opposed to the spread of slavery, but lost. He died at the outset of the Civil War.

Both Jackson and Van Buren claimed their policies towards Native Americans were just and righteous. For the Native Americans, it was quite the opposite. Jackson and Van Buren might not have intended Indian removal to be genocidal, but it was genocidal in practice, nonetheless, because it killed thousands of innocent Native Americans—forced to go through with these marches simply because they were Native American. Jackson is remembered as a strong military leader, and he certainly was, but he treated his allies as badly as his enemies if they were Native American. Jackson and Van Buren's legacy is one in which racism bleeds through every perspective. They were men of the people, but for them, "the people" were only defined as white men. They were populist only because they appealed to and were concerned about the voting population. Slaves, women, non-white immigrants, and Native Americans were to be protected by the benevolence of white men, but that benevolence only stretched so far. If proper money had been set aside and managed by honest men, the Trail of Tears would still have been exceptionally racist, but it at least wouldn't have been so deadly. The responsibility for the deaths of these Native Americans must be placed on someone. And, since those who orchestrated the policy at the highest level wanted acclaim for their actions, they also deserve the responsibility and legacy of their antihumanitarian actions. Every death on the Trail of Tears belongs at the feet of Jackson and Van Buren—and many more deaths besides.

Chapter 8: Indian Removal Act of 1830

At the beginning of the 19th century, the American population was often aptly described as land-hungry. Americans, many newly immigrated from England, Ireland, and Scotland, desired large tracts of land for mostly agricultural pursuits. In the warmer South, planters wanted large areas to grow vast quantities of rice, tobacco, and cotton. In the more temperate North, farmers focused on growing grains and corn. Both areas were used for livestock, especially pork and cattle. Americans continually pushed west into what would become Ohio, Kentucky, West Virginia, Pennsylvania, the Carolinas, Tennessee, Alabama, and Mississippi. The promise of rich soil and prosperity overruled the dangers of native populations or the fact that these Americans were breaking established treaties with various Native American tribes. American colonies, which started at the coasts, invariably continued a steady push westward into the interior. In Ohio, for instance, when the first official American settlement was established in the town of Marietta, there were already scores of families that had settled in that area and been pushed out by Native Americans, only to be replaced by more squatters.

While disease certainly took a toll on Native American populations, it was truly the unending supply of white settlers that sealed the fate of the tribes in these areas more than any technological or imagined societal advances. Both the population growth in the British Isles and the promise of great wealth in the "New World" led to the United States' predictable routine of making treaties only to break them and force Native Americans out of their lands. Some Americans who made these treaties might have believed they would hold, but many must have known they were empty promises. The US leaders had little to no control over the expansion of their country towards the Mississippi River; eventually, this reality would be described as "Manifest Destiny," giving it the implication of something greater than what it was.

At the beginning of the 19th century, it had been enough for the federal government to make treaties with tribes as they saw fit, but by the 1820s, it became apparent to some that there needed to be a standard federal policy dictating how to handle Native American issues. When Jackson won the election of 1828, he already had a new and far-reaching "Indian policy" in mind, with the belief that the Native Americans of the Southeast should give up their lands and move to lands west of the Mississippi River. Former presidents Jefferson and Monroe had expressed a desire to do just that but had never proposed any legislation. Jackson had already done this after the Battle of Horseshoe Bend when he forced the Creek to give up twenty-two million acres in the southeast for twenty-two million acres in what would become Arkansas.

Native Americans had adapted to this new strategy. They recognized that they could not defeat the Americans in battle since they could no longer rely on alliances with European powers like England, France, or Spain to counteract the Americans, who outnumbered them. Instead, the Creek, Cherokee, Choctaw, and Chickasaw thought the best response would be appeasement. These tribes began to conform to American ideals in large numbers. If, they theorized, they surrendered some of their lands to the Americans, then perhaps they could keep some of their homelands and live alongside them. If they looked like Americans, farmed like Americans, were Christians like Americans, and owned slaves like their American neighbors, then perhaps the Americans would hold to their word. Of course, in retrospect, one can see they underestimated how much the Americans desired their lands and how they would never see Native Americans as equals. Still, these tribes had very few options under the circumstances they found themselves in.

The process of the Indian Removal Act was for the president to first establish lands west of the Mississippi and offer allotments of that land to Native American tribes. Those who did not want to go west would be allotted land in their current state and become US citizens subject to US laws. (Jackson believed only the richest landowners among the Native Americans would take this option.) The act provided specific language that gave the president the power to guarantee the land he was giving to the Native Americans would always be theirs. However, if the Native Americans became extinct or abandoned the land, it would revert to US ownership. It also stated that if the land the Native Americans were leaving had been improved by them in any way, the improvements would be given a value, and that value would be paid to them. (This rarely happened.) The president would be required to provide "proper" aid and assistance for Native Americans to emigrate to their new lands and to provide aid and assistance for the first year they occupied their new lands. The act also specified that $500,000 be set aside to help enforce the act as described. (Very little of that money was used to assist the Native Americans.)

On May 26th, 1830, the US House of Representatives voted on the Indian Removal Act. It passed with a narrow vote of 102 for and 97 against. Senator Theodore Frelinghuysen from New Jersey and others strongly opposed the act in the Senate. However, Jackson and his powerful supporters were too much to be reckoned with. The act was quickly passed in the Senate and signed into law by Jackson on May 28th, 1830. In December of that year, Jackson outlined his Indian removal policy in his second annual message, stating that he was happy to announce that the "benevolent policy of the Government" was approaching its end, as he had already removed several Native Americans to land in the west.

Frelinghuysen and his fellows in the Senate were not the only opponents of the Indian Removal Act. Tennessee Representative Davy Crockett openly opposed Indian removal. But the greatest opponents were the Native Americans themselves. As a whole, they did not support removal in any fashion. Some simply saw it as inevitable, but many urged their leaders to fight back, usually through legal means and not militarily, which had already been tried. The lands they were being asked to give up were their ancestral homes—villages, forests, and mountains that had been as much a part of their culture as any ritual or clan. The largest resistant group was the Cherokee, and they would not be completely removed until 1839.

Jackson's Indian Removal Act codified America's goals. When the act passed, Jackson and his administration were free to persuade, bribe, and threaten tribes to give up their land in the Southeast. In the process of enforcing the Indian Removal Act, Jackson signed seventy treaties with

Native Americans, forcing them, eventually, into what would be eastern Oklahoma. By the 1840s, except for the small group of Seminoles fighting in Florida, no Native Americans lived from the Atlantic Coast to the Mississippi River in the American South.

There was an attempt in the Senate to make sure that the quality of the land that the Native Americans were being moved to would be the same as that of the land they were leaving, but this was struck down. Therefore, many Native Americans found the new lands arid and lacking timber and game. Not only that, but the new territory they were sent to was not completely devoid of its own native people. Hence, the process of displacement and violence rippled across the Great Plains.

Still, the language of the Removal Act gave the impression that the Native Americans were being sent to new lands to form their own nations far from white settlers. In 1830, Americans must have realized that the frontier would continue to be pushed west until it reached the Pacific. The idea that white settlers would not cross the Mississippi, often held at the beginning of the 9th century, had long since proven unsound. Missouri had become a state in 1821, after all. Arkansas would enter the union in 1836. In 1839, as the last of the Cherokee were making their way across the Mississippi, the University of Missouri, the first of its kind west of the river, was founded. Indian Territory would remain just that until, finally, in 1907, Oklahoma became the 46th state.

But the Native Americans had wanted something different. They tried as hard as possible to keep their ancestral lands—that was their primary goal. They were willing to live as whites and be accepted into their society as long as they could keep their land. They started newspapers like the *Cherokee Phoenix*, which applauded the ways that the Cherokee and fellow tribes dressed in fine clothes, went to church, and raised livestock. The same issue that the *Cherokee Phoenix* announced the Removal Act also featured a fine review of the Chickasaw, who had abandoned the habit of having women toil in the fields. Instead, the men worked in the fields while the women of the family stayed home and were occupied with domestic affairs. The Chickasaw horses were described as stronger and more resilient than the horses of white men. But it was not enough. Native Americans could look and act the part—even exceeding the whites in certain aspect—but they wouldn't be accepted into American society. The Americans, at least those with the most power, would only be happy if Native Americans were completely and utterly removed.

Chapter 9: The Treaty of New Echota

In 1790, a part Scot, part Cherokee child named John Ross was born in Alabama. He grew up learning Cherokee culture from his mother and maternal grandmother and also received a fine education in schools in Tennessee, where his family lived. He urged the Cherokee to ally themselves with the United States in the Creek War with the Red Sticks. Ross joined the fight and was an adjunct of a Cherokee unit under the command of Andrew Jackson. After the war, he started a plantation in Tennessee growing tobacco. He built a warehouse and started a ferry service from the Cherokee side to the US side of the Tennessee River. The community that grew up around his land was called Ross' Landing. This town would eventually become Chattanooga. He also began to take part in Cherokee politics. In 1816, he traveled to Washington, DC, as part of a delegation to negotiate boundaries and white encroachment. By 1828, he was elected to be the principal chief of the Cherokee Nation. At that time, the Cherokee had written a constitution, formed a national council and courts, and established a capital at New Echota in Georgia. Other Cherokee leaders at the time included Elias Boudinot and John Ridge.

Since the 1820s, the Cherokee had a written language and their own newspaper published in both English and Cherokee. By 1830, many Cherokee could read and write. Missionaries within the Nation provided Christian-English education, as well. Federal programs provided many Cherokee with tools and training so that they could farm their land in the same manner as whites. The Cherokee were businessmen, farmers, slaveholders, and traders. They owned taverns or, like Ross, ferries. They had shown themselves to be firm allies of the United States over the previous three decades.

Still, it was not enough to appease their neighbors. White Americans could not tell the difference between friendly Native Americans and enemies. They distrusted the entire race of Native Americans and coveted their fertile lands and hunting grounds. Many Americans held onto the stories of the attack on Fort Mims and other actions taken by the Red Sticks in the 1810s and wrongly believed the Cherokee were involved, even though the Cherokee fought against the Red Sticks under the command of Jackson.

The already tense situation worsened when gold was found in Dahlonega, Lumpkin County, Georgia, seventy miles from New Echota. Americans, especially in the state of Georgia, wanted the land on which the gold was found, and they certainly wanted the gold itself. Despite the gold being on Cherokee land, white people began to pour into the region and set up individual mining operations, typically placer mining, in which a rocker box or sluice box is used to sift sand in a stream bed. Finding gold was not the primary reason that Georgia wanted to remove the Cherokee from its borders, but it was one.

With this in mind, Georgia passed a new law in 1828 that would take effect in 1830. It annexed all Cherokee land within the borders of Georgia, made null and void all Cherokee laws, and forbade anyone with Native American blood from bearing witness in a trial against a white man. Before the new law came into effect, Congress passed the Indian Removal Act. When that bill passed, Georgia also passed a bill saying that the Cherokee could not take any gold from their land. Georgia's Governor Gilmer claimed that the state owned the title to the Cherokee land, including all mineral rights. Georgia also passed laws to stop the Cherokee Tribal Council from meeting within the state. In 1831, surveyors entered Cherokee territory and began to split the land up into 160-acre lots and 40-acre gold lots. These were then given away in a statewide lottery. Prominent Cherokees like John Ross and the wealthy Joseph Vann were kicked off their property by the lottery winners. However, land belonging to pro-removal Cherokee was left out of the lottery. In 1834, this included Elias Boudinot and John Ridge.

Council meetings were relocated to Tennessee, where many Cherokee moved after Georgia had taken away their land. John Ross moved to Red Hill, where the council met, and Vann left his Georgia plantation for the home he already owned in Tennessee. Many missionaries remained on Cherokee lands in Georgia, which was technically illegal, and were arrested. Most of them submitted to state authorities, but two, Elizur Butler and Samuel Worcester, did not and were sentenced to four years of hard labor. In the Supreme Court's 1832 decision in *Worcester v. Georgia*, the court declared that the Cherokee Nation was sovereign and that Georgia's laws were null and void.

Upon hearing the news, John Ridge asked for a personal audience with President Jackson to determine how the president would proceed. If Ridge had been hopeful of the court's decision, he was soon brought back to Earth when Jackson informed him in no uncertain terms that he would do nothing to enforce the court's verdict. Jackson told Ridge that the only hope for his people was removal. Before this, it is believed Ridge had been against removal, but after this meeting, some contend he changed his position. Ridge denied this, but Jackson reported to a friend that Ridge had left the audience in obvious despair. Ridge had been part of a delegation in Washington, and before the delegation returned home, rumors were everywhere that the delegation members were considering removal. They denied the accusations, but Ridge received a letter not much later from the American Board of Commissioners for Foreign Missions telling him that the Cherokee cause was hopeless, the Supreme Court decision was useless, and that they must enter into a treaty of removal.

After this, a rift developed within the Cherokee Nation. One side, the Treaty Party, which included John Ridge, his son John, and Elias Boudinot, supported the idea of negotiating a treaty, including removal. Boudinot, editor of the *Cherokee Phoenix*, resigned because he was not allowed to print arguments for removal. John Ross and his supporters came to be known as the National Party; they were strictly against any form of removal. By 1834, tensions had grown to the point of violence. In August, John Walker, Jr. was shot as he returned home from a council meeting, supposedly because of his pro-removal views.

In the fall of that year, the two sides held separate council meetings. The Treaty Party drew up a resolution that explained that they felt the best option for their people was removal. The US War Department ignored the National Party and dealt only with the Treaty Party. Ross, however, persisted in demanding to be heard by the US government. His party was kept in negotiations into 1835. In the meantime, an emissary from the US War Department named Schermerhorn proposed a new council in New Echota in December of 1835. Boudinot and Ridge were invited, but they told Schermerhorn that few Cherokee would attend. In October, the Georgia National Guard raided John Ross' house and arrested him. He was held for twelve days and then released without explanation.

In December, Ridge, Boudinot, and 300–400 Cherokee arrived in New Echota. Twenty Cherokee men did most of the negotiating, and on December 29th, 1835, they signed or made their mark on the Treaty of New Echota. It ceded the Cherokee lands in the east for $5 million plus the cost of emigration and land west of the Mississippi. Among the signers were John Ridge, his son, and Elias Boudinot. The treaty was ratified by Congress in May of 1836. The treaty stipulated that the Cherokee had two years to move from their lands in Georgia, Tennessee, North Carolina, and Alabama. It also said that any Native Americans who wanted to remain in the East could become US citizens and would be allotted 160 acres in their ancestral lands, except for Georgia. As soon as word of the treaty came out, the US Government sent troops to police and disarm the Cherokee in case of any resistance. Ross kept his supporters calm and attempted to overturn the treaty. He sent a petition with signatures representing 16,000 Cherokee who opposed the Treaty of New Echota. General Wool, in charge of the US troops, forwarded the protests to President Jackson, who disparaged Wool, saying that sending those protests was disrespectful to the president. There were now no options left for the Cherokee. Removal had become a reality.

Chapter 10: The Trail of Tears

To speak of the "Trail of Tears" implies that there was only one trail and perhaps only one instance. This gives the general audience the idea that it might have been accidental when, in fact, there were several trails over many years. The US government had sought the removal of Native Americans in the East to lands in the West many times, which often involved a deadly march for large numbers of people, who were mainly on foot and trudging through harsh conditions without proper supplies. The Creek, Chickasaw, Choctaw, and Seminole were all removed to lands west of the Mississippi River. Many scores died from disease, exhaustion, exposure, and malnutrition.

By 1837, when the first group of Cherokee after the signing of the Treaty of New Echota were to be marched west, the US War Department and the Bureau of Indian Affairs had already conducted such marches many times over. They felt they were well prepared for what was to come; any mistakes that had been made were surely resolved by that time. There were already, in fact, some Cherokee living in Indian Territory when the infamous Treaty of New Echota was signed. After a census was taken, it was decided that about 4,000 Cherokee men, women, and children needed to be removed. This was certainly a large number, but the US forces involved had received plenty of training and real-life experience of the horrors of marching civilians over rough terrain. They should have known, one could reason, just how much food, water, blankets, and so on would be needed. They could have foreseen the dangers in such a march and planned for them. Yet, if that were the case, how can we explain the eventual outcome of the "Trail of Tears"?

The first group of Cherokee to leave set out on the first of the year 1837. It consisted of 600 individuals from the Treaty Party, mostly what might be considered middle or upper-middle-class. Taking slaves, horses, and oxen with them, they followed a route from Tennessee through Kentucky, Illinois, Missouri, and Arkansas. There were no deaths reported on this journey.

Major John Ridge and his family, along with eighteen slaves, left in March. With them were almost 500 emigrants under the direction of Dr. John S. Young. This was a government-run operation. They traveled by steamboats, which hauled flatboats, and also by train. Four deaths were reported. Several emigrants were ill, but they were cared for by two doctors who traveled with the group. They arrived after a few weeks.

Elias Boudinot and a group emigrated via horse and wagon, traveling through Nashville. They arrived without any deaths.

The deadline for removal—May 23, 1838—arrived, and two thousand Cherokee had left for the west, many of them from the Treaty Party. John Ross continued to work to get the New Echota Treaty nullified or overturned, but it came to no avail. General Wool had been replaced by Colonel Lindsay, who was then replaced by General Winfield Scott. When the deadline was reached, Scott began giving orders to commence the removal. It was not vague. In his orders, he told every commander to round up as many Cherokees as possible and bring the "prisoners" to emigrating depots at key locations. He explained that these operations were to be repeated over and over until the entire Cherokee Nation had collected for emigration.

Two thousand soldiers were under Scott's command, including two artillery regiments. The Cherokee were pulled from their homes and fields, sometimes at gunpoint, and forcibly marched from temporary camps to depots. Scott ordered his troops to go about their duties as humanely as possible, without undue violence. All the same, the Cherokee reported that soldiers burst into their homes in the middle of their supper and forced them outside at the end of a bayonet. Soldiers were told to enter every cabin and every building in search of prisoners. The Cherokee had to leave their belongings behind; these were gathered up days after the families had left and put into wagons with little regard for what came from which household.

In June of 1838, over 4,000 Cherokee had been gathered at Ross' Landing, one of the emigration depots, to be sent west. The first group was ordered at gunpoint to board steamboats and flatboats headed to Decatur, Alabama. There they boarded trains and then steamboats, which traveled north on the Tennessee River to Paducah, Kentucky. On the boats, the Cherokee were subject to the elements, and on land, they had no means of camping since they did not have time to prepare for their sudden departure. Many had been holding out hope that the Treaty of New Echota could be overturned; some had even rejected offers of blankets for fear that it would be taken as a sign of acceptance of the dreaded treaty. Some of the Cherokee were provided with cotton sheets to make tents. One commander described them as in "destitute condition"—this was a party of 600 that had not yet suffered a death.

A group of 876 Cherokee had traveled by boat to Morrilton, Arkansas, but were forced to walk the remaining 1,554 miles because the rivers were too low to carry the boats. Seventy-three people died on this march, and approximately 208 deserted along the way. Half of another group of over a thousand had tried to desert at once. Troops were mustered to round up the deserters, and they captured all but 255. At least 150 died during this ill-fated march. Two women gave birth during the journey. The Cherokees who remained in the emigration camps faced dreadful conditions, as well, as disease spread through them with ferocity. On June 19, 1838, General Scott ordered that the emigrations should be temporarily postponed due to the heat and sickness that was killing the emigrating Cherokee. The Tribal Council sent a message to Scott, asking that he continue their removal. Scott, whose fast and humane removal plan had proved impossible, agreed but told the council they had to wait until September. John Ross was chosen to organize this self-removal and asked for $65.88 for each person to provide food, shelter, other necessities, and provisions for their livestock. Scott agreed, though he considered the request for soap too lavish.

During the summer, more and more Cherokee, including some Creek, were amassed at temporary camps, largely in Tennessee. These camps were crowded, though they were expanded to allow more privacy. Occasionally, some natives were let out of the camps to hunt. Plenty of Cherokee tried to escape, many returning to their old homes only to be rounded up by troops again. The summer wore on, and camps were often moved, possibly because water sources had become polluted. By July, Scott was issuing 7, 217 daily rations. The officers under Scott became concerned for the welfare of the Cherokee. People were allowed to travel between camps to find family members, vaccines were given to fight disease, and large stations were set up to make the delivery of rations easier. Still, reports indicate numerous cases of diarrhea, dysentery, measles, and whooping cough spread through the camps. While physicians were assigned to the camps, their work was difficult because they lacked interpreters to assist them and help administer medicine. This made treating the sick a time-consuming ordeal.

When September finally came, the Cherokee were moved into groups of a thousand or fewer, but the going was hard. A drought had hit the area and made moving by boat impossible in some cases. It took months to make their way to the Mississippi, and by then, a harsh winter had set in. Many rivers were impassable due to floating ice, although some could be crossed because they had frozen solid. Many Cherokee died from disease and malnutrition on the way, most noticeably scores of children. As they waited for floating ice to clear from the Mississippi, heavy snow began to fall, and their small tents must have seemed very meager to the warm cabins they had been forced from several months before.

While these last emigrations were conducted by the designs of the Cherokee themselves, led by Chief John Ross, they were still hampered by the US Army commanders, who told them when they could move and made many decisions about the paths they would take. They did not have the option of turning back at any point, and they could not wait too long for a change in the season. They needed to press on with haste to Indian Territory. By March of 1839, the Cherokee had crossed the Mississippi River and were traveling through Arkansas to their new land. One of the doctors assigned to Lt. Whiteley's group kept a record of the journey through Arkansas. March was filled with reports of severe cold and snow. The country they traveled through was barren; the doctor sometimes called it a desert. By March 24, 1839, the Cherokees of his detachment were "handed over to the government" and settled in their new lands. It would be June of that year before the last of the Cherokee led by Chief Ross entered Indian Territory.

The numbers are uncertain, but estimates indicate about 5,000 Cherokee died on the Trail of Tears. That number increases by several thousand when including the Choctaw, Creek, Chickasaw, and Seminole, and does not include the tribes removed from the North, such as the Sauk and Fox. It is believed that 3,500 of the 15,000 Creek who were removed died on their Trail of Tears. The impact of these forced migrations cannot be easily comprehended. Families were forced from their homes by soldiers with rifles armed with bayonets; if they resisted, they could be killed. The story of Tsali from the Eastern Cherokee involves a family who fought back against the soldiers, and two soldiers were killed in the scuffle. Tsali was the old patriarch of the family, and they fled into the mountains of North Carolina. General Scott demanded their capture. The story varies, but it seems that Tsali, his brother, and the two eldest sons were either captured or surrendered themselves and were summarily shot. Their deaths were meant to be a lesson to any Cherokee who considered resisting removal.

Each group's trail or trails were different, some swift and without incident and others trials of will in which hundreds died. Weather, disease, and fatigue seemed to haunt the Cherokees on these journeys. Whites along the way would refuse to help them and sometimes assault them. Missionaries, doctors, and soldiers that traveled with the Cherokee were even refused accommodations at some of their stops simply because they were with the hated group. It must have felt as if the world was conspiring to destroy them, and how they must have suffered through these terrible months is beyond understanding. The fact that many survived and made the best of their new and foreign circumstances is a credit to their nations.

SECTION THREE:
RESISTANCE AND OPPOSITION

Chapter 11: Tippecanoe and the Early Creek Wars

Governor Arthur St. Clair.
https://commons.wikimedia.org/wiki/File:ArthurStClairOfficialPortrait-restored.jpg

The Battle of Tippecanoe

In 1790, Arthur St. Clair had good reason to feel confident. Born in Scotland, he had joined the British Army and been stationed in North America. He liked his new home and friends so much that when America rebelled, he was on the side of the Patriots. He joined the revolutionary cause and rose through the ranks quickly. When General Washington was facing the British in Trenton, it was St. Clair who had suggested taking Princeton and outflanking the British. Washington supported St. Clair for the rest of the war and listened carefully to the soldier's opinions. St. Clair eventually became a major general, and when the war was won, he served as the first president of the Continental Congress. Part of the Treaty of Paris between England and the new United States was that America now owned what was known as the Northwest Territory, a large tract of land that would eventually become Ohio, Indiana, Michigan, Illinois, and Wisconsin. St. Clair was promptly made the governor of the Northwest Territory.

The US government had sold the Northwest Territory to land speculators to recoup some of the cost of the revolution. These speculators, which were often companies of shareholders (including St. Clair), had bought the land with the belief that they could turn around and sell it to settlers for a profit. Plenty of Americans desired to buy the land and farm it, in turn making a profit from growing corn, grain, or livestock. Ohio Country, in particular, showed signs of being very fertile and accommodating to agriculture. There was also the beautiful Ohio River that could carry traffic down to the Mississippi, New Orleans, and even to the Caribbean. The only thing stopping this from moving forward was the "Indian Problem."

When Americans ventured into the territory, they often met resistance from the Native Americans who lived there. Violence broke out on both sides and made the area a dangerous place, diminishing the settlers that St. Clair and many others desired. With this in mind, St. Clair had called a meeting at Fort Harmar in 1788 to settle a treaty that would firmly establish that the Native Americans would leave the Ohio Country for good. At the meeting were representatives from the Wyandot, the Lenape, the Ottawa, the Chippewa, the Potawatomi, and the Sauk. St. Clair first threatened those gathered that the US Army would attack them if they did not comply. He then bribed them with thousands of dollars in gifts. The Native Americans there signed the Treaty of Fort Harmar. The issues that arose came largely from the fact that not all the tribes of the area were represented; specifically, there was no one there to represent the Miami and the Shawnee.

The Native Americans responded by attacking the new settlements and forts built under the treaty. An expedition was led by General Harmar against the Native Americans, which was severely defeated. In 1790, St. Clair took the command himself. He led 1,400 men deep into the wilderness to subdue and defeat the Shawnee, Miami, and their Lenape allies. President Washington had warned St. Clair to be wary of surprise attacks, and he must have believed he was more than prepared for the battle. But when the battle came, he was not. In a surprise attack, the Miami, Shawnee, and Lenape succeeded in wounding or killing 900 of St. Clair's men. Only a last-minute bayonet charge led by St. Clair himself stopped what some called a massacre. The battle would be remembered as "St. Clair's Defeat" and would be the worst defeat of the US Army at the hands of Native Americans. President Washington called St. Clair "worse than a murderer," and his office investigated the matter. St. Clair was acquitted, but he was relieved of his command. However, he remained governor of the Northwest Territory until Jefferson removed him. He never recovered his investment in Ohio Country and lived out the rest of his days in a small cabin in Western Pennsylvania.

The Native Americans that defeated St. Clair's forces that November day were led by Little Turtle of the Miami and Blue Jacket of the Shawnee. One young Shawnee warrior had missed the fighting that day because he had been out scouting or hunting. He had only recently returned to Ohio Country after moving first to Missouri and then Tennessee. While away, he had heard the teaching of Mohawk Chief Joseph Brant, who believed that Native American lands should only be ceded if every tribe agreed and that they should present a unified front against US expansion. This young warrior, whose mother might have been Creek and who had a daughter with a Cherokee woman, agreed with Brant's teaching. He had tried to move away from white settlements, but everywhere he went, he found white settlers. So, he was back in Ohio and ready to fight. His name, which means something like "Shooting Star," comes to us as Tecumseh.

After St. Clair's stunning defeat, Washington and Secretary of War Knox recognized that the organization of what had been the Continental Army needed to drastically change to deal with the threat of united Native American forces in the Northwest. Their solution was the Legion of the United States, a new professional army that could more easily adapt to the changing circumstances in Ohio Country. They picked Major General "Mad" Anthony Wayne to lead this new army. Wayne was a Revolutionary

War hero from Pennsylvania who was proven capable of tactical brilliance. Secretary Knox made sure Wayne had enough soldiers, cannons, and supplies to subdue the Native Americans. Wayne, learning from St. Clair's mistakes, trained his troops hard before taking them into the wilderness. During the Revolutionary War, Wayne's troops had been surprised by a night attack from the British, and Wayne was determined not to be surprised in such a way again. After two years of training, focusing on building defenses, marksmanship, and close-quarter combat, Wayne felt that his legion was ready to fight. The Legion traveled north, founding forts along the way.

The Native Americans, led by Blue Jacket, planned to ambush Wayne's forces in a clearing known as Fallen Timbers. Among the warriors there was Tecumseh. But Wayne's extensive training had paid off. His scouts had alerted him to the ambush, and his troops had charged the Miami and Shawnee hiding positions and flushed the warriors out. This time, the Native Americans were surprised. Many turned and ran in the face of the Legion's musket fire. The Battle of Fallen Timbers lasted less than an hour and proved to be a rout. The Native Americans had been hoping for support from nearby British allies, but none was given. The British were not yet ready to engage in another war with the United States. The defeat was devastating to the Native Americans. In 1795, Wayne organized the Treaty of Greenville, in which Little Turtle and Blue Jacket agreed to cede a large portion of Ohio Country to the United States. Another treaty, the Treaty of Fort Industry, signed in 1805, gave even more of Ohio to the US. Tecumseh sharply criticized the "peace chiefs" who had signed away so much of his tribe's homeland.

Tecumseh was soon a great chief himself, and he planned a grand alliance of all Native Americans to stop the spread of white settlers. He was assisted by his younger brother. Born Lalawethika, this younger brother had been unskilled at hunting and fighting and had taken to alcohol. Then, one day, he fell into a trance, and his family believed he had died. When he regained consciousness, he told them he had been given a divine vision. The "Master of Life" had told him that the Native Americans needed to give up the use of white goods, return to traditional ways, and drive the Americans out of their land. He also told him he would now be known as Tenskwatawa, the "Prophet." Tecumseh believed in his brother's vision, and together they founded Prophetstown in what would eventually be Tippecanoe County, Indiana.

In early November 1811, Governor William Henry Harrison led 1,000 troops to Prophetstown to end Tecumseh's alliance. Luckily for Harrison, Tecumseh was not in Prophetstown at the time. He had ventured south hoping to gain the alliance of the Five Civilized Tribes.

Only Tenskwatawa and 500 warriors were there to defend their new capital. When Harrison arrived, a warrior carrying a white flag came out to ask for a cease-fire so that Harrison and Tecumseh could parley. Harrison agreed to the terms but was weary. Tecumseh had told his brother not to enter into battle until their alliance was stronger, but the Prophet disregarded the warning. On the morning of November 7, Tenskwatawa surrounded Harrison's men and attacked. It was a bold move, but it did not pay off. Harrison's superior numbers and firepower proved more than enough to defeat the Native American alliance army. The Prophet had promised the warriors that the American bullets would not hurt them, but when they were defeated, they abandoned Tenskwatawa and Prophetstown. This allowed Harrison to raid and destroy the town.

When Tecumseh returned three months later, his dream had already been crushed. The Cherokee had turned down his offer of an alliance, and only a few Creek were moved by his words. His brother's foolhardy actions had led to a great loss he could not prevent. This left Tecumseh with only one option: to ally himself with the British, just as Little Turtle and Blue Jacket had done. The defeat at the Battle of Tippecanoe forced Tecumseh's hand. When the War of 1812 broke out, he found himself relying on the promises of white Europeans to protect his land and people from white Americans. It was certainly not what he had hoped for.

Early Creek Wars

Tecumseh's arrival and message in 1811 caused a rift in the Creek Nation. The Red Sticks vied for control of the Creek, and a civil war erupted. The Americans became involved in this southern conflict while also fighting Tecumseh and the British in the Northwest in the War of 1812. Not only that, but the British were attacking the American coastline and would even take Washington, DC, and burn down the White House. America was concerned that the British and possibly the Spanish were arming the Red Sticks, and this fear proved correct. The Red Sticks were attacked by the Americans returning from Spanish-controlled Florida. Partly in retaliation to this, they famously attacked Fort Sims, where they killed hundreds of men, women, and children. The actions of the Red Sticks were not particularly brutal compared to other attacks by US forces or other Native Americans. Americans had killed scores of civilians, and the colonists had done the same before them, not to mention capturing and enslaving thousands. This was a total war, with the intent of breaking the enemy and keeping them from expanding into Native American territory. However, the attack on Fort Mims became a rallying cry for the white settlers in Alabama, Georgia, Tennessee, Mississippi, and the Carolinas. It struck directly at the fear that so many settlers felt about the threat that Native Americans posed. Instead of convincing the settlers to make peace, it only made them want to avenge those killed at Fort Mims. They did not seem to care that many of those killed in the massacre were part Native American.

This was when Major General Andrew Jackson stepped onto the national stage to play his part as the man who would defeat the "Indian Menace." Unlike Anthony Wayne, Jackson was not leading professional soldiers but militiamen who signed up for a few months of fighting. He knew he had to act quickly. Two months after the attack on Fort Mims, one of Jackson's cavalry units destroyed the Red Stick town of Tallushatchee. Jackson then attacked Talladega and scored another victory against forces led by the Red Stick Chief William Weatherford, who might have been related to Tecumseh. Georgia militia under Brig. Gen. John Floyd attacked the towns of Autossee and Tallassee. Then the Mississippian militia attacked the Holy Ground with the help of the Cherokee led by Chief Pushmataha.

By January of 1814, Jackson was heading towards the Red Stick's main town, Tohopeka. The Red Sticks met him at Horseshoe Bend; he repulsed their attack but was forced to withdraw. Returning in March, he found the Red Sticks well fortified. He led a frontal assault while part of his cavalry, allied Creek, and Cherokee outflanked the Red Sticks. Jackson's forces were victorious. Many of the Red Sticks who survived the battle fled into Florida, where they joined the Creek already there (the Seminole). Jackson had those who remained sign the Treaty of Fort Jackson, which handed over twenty-three million acres of Creek land. The Creek war of 1813-1814 had ended. The Creek who allied with the Americans were treated the same as the Red Sticks; no distinction was made in the peace that followed.

Chapter 12: The Seminole Trilogy and the Black Hawk War

The First Seminole War

By 1817, the Seminole were a distinct Native American people of largely Creek origin living in Northern Florida. Alongside them also lived Africans, free African Americans, and escaped African American slaves, who were collectively known as Black Seminole. The Seminole and Black Seminole had allied with the British in the War of 1812. Because of this and the presence of freedom-seeking slaves, Northern Florida villages were subject to constant raids by Georgia whites who wanted to capture runaway slaves and take land and cattle from the Seminole, who they viewed as an enemy. These raids were sometimes conducted by state militia and organized by state leaders. In 1816, American troops killed 270 people when they destroyed the Negro Fort in the Battle of Prospect Bluff. In response, the Seminole began to raid Georgia.

The First Seminole War began in 1817 when American soldiers attacked and destroyed the Seminole town of Fowltown. This was after the dispute between the Seminole and the commander of Fort Scott concerning land ownership and who was subject to the Treaty of Fort Jackson. The Seminole responded by attacking a boat on the Apalachicola River, killing forty-three.

General Jackson was then given command of the forces in the South. In 1818, he entered Florida and began destroying Seminole towns as he went. He took the Spanish fort at St. Marks, then set his sights on the Spanish-owned city of Pensacola. He knew that Spanish and British forces were there helping the Seminole and Black Seminole, so he wanted to deal a decisive blow that would end the conflict. Jackson had about 4,000 men. In Pensacola, there were 100 British, 500 Spanish, and an unknown number of Seminole warriors. Jackson's superior numbers won the day, and the Spanish governor soon surrendered. The British also hastily left the city. Jackson agreed not to destroy the city when he took it.

This effectively ended the First Seminole War and led to Spain ceding Florida in 1821 to the United States under the Adams-Onís Treaty. As soon as the US gained control of Florida, it began to demand that the Seminole leave the peninsula and go to Indian Territory in Oklahoma. Eventually, some Seminole signed the Treaty of Payne's Landing in 1832, agreeing to removal. Some of the tribe then left and went too far-off Indian Territory. However, some Seminole refused to sign the treaty and fled into the Florida Everglades.

The Second Seminole War

The Treaty of Payne's Landing gave the Seminole three years to prepare for removal. When the US Army arrived in 1835 to enforce the treaty, many Seminole were prepared to fight. The Second Seminole War lasted from 1835 to 1842 and was, perhaps, the fiercest war fought between the United States and Native Americans. It was a lesson in guerilla warfare as four Seminole chiefs (*micos*) with only 3,000 warriors faced off against four US generals who commanded around 30,000 troops.

On December 28, 1835, Seminole under the command of Mico Osceola attacked and killed General Wiley Thompson outside Fort King. The same day, 300 Seminole ambushed troops under the command of Major Francis Dade. Two years later, Colonel Zachary Taylor and 1,100 troops were ambushed by 400 Seminole. Twenty-six US troops were killed and 112 wounded in the Seminole's carefully-planned trap. Between these two ambushes, the Seminole continually harassed the US Army forces attempting to forcibly remove the Seminole from Florida. In the summer of 1837, Osceola was captured under a false flag of truce. If the US commanders believed this would end hostilities, they were wrong. The Seminole fought on even after Osceola died in captivity in January of 1838. By 1842, the US had captured most of the Seminole and sent them to Indian Territory. Hostilities came to an end without the signing of a treaty.

Third Seminole War

The final Seminole War began in 1855 and was primarily about conflicts between whites and Seminole over land. The US Army maintained patrols in the region and also offered rewards for the capture of Seminole. This led to the remaining population of Seminole in Florida totaling no more than 200 individuals by 1858 and would mark the end of the final Seminole War.

Black Hawk War

In April of 1832, a group of one thousand Native Americans crossed the Mississippi River and headed east into Illinois—the opposite direction of the Trail of Tears. The group was composed of members of the Sauk, Fox, and Kickapoo tribes. They were led by a sixty-five-year-old Sauk chief named Black Hawk. This chief had led his people for fifty years, fighting their many enemies, including the Americans. However, in his old age, Black Hawk was not looking for war when he led his people into northern Illinois past the ruined remains of the once-great Sauk village of Saukenuk, which was by then home to a few white settlers. Black Hawk was in search of something like retirement, but it was not to be. The presence of Black Hawk's group caused a great deal of anxiety for the white settlers in the area. The group was soon pursued by the US Army and Illinois militia, as well as Sioux and Menominee warriors.

Black Hawk's band was headed towards Prophetstown, Illinois. This was the village of one of Black Hawk's advisers, White Cloud, also known as the Winnebago Prophet. White Cloud had told Black Hawk that the British would ally with him against the Americans. Seeing that their situation was untenable, Black Hawk's band turned around and attempted to re-cross the Mississippi, but an engagement with a militia group hindered their retreat. What followed was a series of skirmishes between the Native Americans and small groups of army or militia. Finally, on July 21, the pursuers caught up to Black Hawk at the Battle of Wisconsin Heights. This would be the main battle in this short-lived war. It occurred near what is today Sauk City, Wisconsin.

There were around 700 militiamen under the command of Colonel Henry Dodge, along with allied Native Americans. Black Hawk's band had nowhere near this many warriors and contained many women and children. Still, the warriors were able to fend off the militia long enough to allow most of the Sauk and Fox to escape. The militia eventually caught up with them on August 1 at the mouth of the Bad Axe River while the band tried to cross the Mississippi.

Two days of battle ensued, and historians refer to the event as the Bad Axe Massacre because of the brutal victory the Americans inflicted on Black Hawk's people. It was the final battle in the Black Hawk War and ensured that Illinois would be free of Native Americans. Black Hawk and White Cloud surrendered to Lt. Jefferson Davis.

As prisoners, Black Hawk, White Cloud, and other leaders were eventually taken east on President Jackson's orders, with the hope of impressing them with the power of the United States. They were taken by steamboat and railroad all around the country and met by large crowds. On the East Coast, Americans seemed mostly curious, but in places like Detroit, the Sauk and Fox leaders were met with threats of violence. Black Hawk was returned to his people and lived with the Sauk in what would become Iowa for the remainder of his days. He died in 1838 of a long illness. His remains were stolen less than a year after his death but were recovered by his son with the help of Governor Robert Lucas of Iowa Territory. The skeleton was then displayed in the building of the Burlington Historical Society. When the building burned down, Black Hawk's remains were destroyed.

Chapter 13: Sand Creek Massacre and Red Cloud's War

Sand Creek Massacre

In the summer of 1864, the governor of Colorado Territory sent out a proclamation that the "friendly" Native Americans of the Cheyenne and Arapaho should report to Fort Lyon in the southeastern part of the territory. The Native Americans were to go to the fort for supplies and safety, but this proclamation directly conflicted with an earlier proclamation stating that any Native American approaching a fort in Colorado should be considered hostile and shot. This obviously caused consternation for the Cheyenne and Arapaho, so their chiefs, including Black Kettle and Little Bear, brought 750 people to camp near Fort Lyon. Black Kettle attempted to make peace with Governor John Evans and Col. John Chivington, who was at Fort Lyon. Black Kettle's camp was mostly made up of women, children, and the elderly. They stayed near Fort Lyon according to the command of the US Army.

One of the officers at Fort Lyon was Captain Silas S. Soule, a hard-fighting gentleman abolitionist originally from Maine. Soule had moved to Kansas and then Colorado, joining the army when the Civil War broke out. He had fought with the Colorado 1st Regiment of Volunteers in the Union victory at Glorieta Pass in New Mexico. The 1st Regiment was then stationed throughout Colorado Territory. Chivington had promoted Soule to captain and assigned him to Fort Lyon.

According to a letter Soule would later write about the incident, Chivington and the 3rd Regiment arrived, arrested two officers at the fort, and declared their intentions to kill the entire party of Cheyenne and Arapaho camped near the fort. Soule was shocked. These Native Americans were peaceful and friendly and had almost no warriors among them; the camp was composed of those who couldn't fight. Soule told anyone who would listen that it would be a cowardly act. His words were returned to Chivington, and some expressed the wish that Soule be hanged for his insubordination.

On November 29, 1864, elements of the 1st and 3rd Regiments approached the camp of Black Kettle's people. Captain Soule was among them, but he had ordered his unit not to fire or engage in battle unless forced. However, under the direction of Colonel Chivington, several units formed a circle around the encampment and opened fire, including artillery fire. Soule was horrified by what he witnessed. Women and children ran out begging for mercy and were shot without provocation. A few men grabbed bows and rifles and tried to defend themselves, but it was useless. Soule described it as a "slaughter." Soule's company was the only one to keep formation and not fire a shot.

The other soldiers were let loose and began killing with reckless abandon and mutilating the corpses. Soule's description is exceptionally graphic. They scalped many bodies and cut off body parts to retrieve jewelry or as souvenirs. This violence continued for six to eight hours. Captain Soules simply stood in silence, bearing witness to the events as they unfolded. He was relieved to see that many of the tribespeople were able to escape to the Cheyenne camp on Smoky Hill River. The total number of Native Americans killed was not clear. Chivington claimed 500 to 600 were killed, while others said it was closer to 140. Only twenty-four US soldiers were killed, and it is believed many of these were due to friendly fire. Eight Cheyenne leaders were killed in the massacre.

Many of the Cheyenne and Arapaho were convinced by militant warrior societies, like the Dog Soldiers, that seeking peace with the whites was folly. Black Kettle, who survived the massacre, continued to advocate peace, but the Dog Soldiers took it upon themselves to retaliate and avenge the murders at Sand Creek. A series of raids and attacks followed in and around Julesburg, Colorado. They then set out for the Black Hills.

Investigations were conducted into the actions of November 29, two by the military and one by the Joint Committee on the Conduct of War.

Captain Soule testified against Chivington, and the panel declared that Chivington had acted in a deplorable manner unbecoming an officer of the US Army. Soule was not the only witness—Lt. James Cannon echoed Soule's accounts with his eyewitness testimony of the atrocities committed by the soldiers and officers at Sand Creek. Chivington was not punished for his role but resigned from the army shortly after the massacre. Afterward, he roamed around the country, often skipping out on debts and infamously seducing his daughter-in-law. He died in 1894, consistent with his belief that his actions were justified at Sand Creek. Captain Silas Soule did not live as long. In April of 1865, just a few months after testifying against Chivington, Soule was murdered while acting as a provost marshal in Denver. He was shot and died before help could arrive. One of his killers was known and brought to justice but was able to avoid a trial and then fled Colorado.

Red Cloud's War

Red Cloud.
https://commons.wikimedia.org/wiki/File:Red_Cloud,_1905,_Felix_Flying_Hawk.jpg

Survivors of the Sand Creek Massacre went to the Powder River Basin in the Black Hills area. Through this area, whites had established a trail that led from the East to southern Montana gold fields; it was called the Bozeman Trail after frontiersman John Bozeman. In 1865, Cheyenne, Oglala Lakota, and Arapaho set up large camps along the Powder and

Tongue Rivers in northern Wyoming Territory. They did not like whites traveling through their land. So, on July 26, 1865, a group attacked Platte Bridge Station, killing twenty-six men.

In response to the growing tensions and this attack, the US War Department sent Col. Henry B. Carrington with 700 troops to subdue the Native Americans in the Powder River area. This angered many Native Americans, including Oglala leader Red Cloud, who was joined by Cheyenne and Arapaho warriors to launch a series of attacks and skirmishes known as Red Cloud's War. Red Cloud and another Sioux leader, Crazy Horse, led Lakota warriors, who trapped and killed eighty US soldiers. In the summer of 1867, Red Cloud and Crazy Horse attacked a woodcutting party with armed protection near Fort Phil Kearney. This, however, was not a massacre. The party quickly built fortifications out of boxes and used their new Springfield-Allen breech-loading rifles, which could load much faster than any weapons the Native Americans had. Only four US soldiers were killed, while the Native Americans counted six dead.

At the same time, the US Department of the Interior was trying to engage in peace talks in that region. The US government had originally said they only wanted safe passage on the Bozeman Trail and peace at the forts they built along the trail. But matters were complicated when the Union Pacific Railroad wanted to build rail lines through the area and expected their workers to be protected by the US Army. Red Cloud wanted the whites to abandon the Bozeman Trail and the forts in the Lakota territory.

The US government was willing to negotiate. At the end of the Civil War, the US Army had been drastically reduced. It was spread over a much larger territory and required to protect Black voting rights at the polls. Also, with the completion of the Union Pacific line, the Bozeman trail had become obsolete. Gold miners and prospectors could simply take the railroad through the disputed land, and there was no longer a need to maintain forts in the area. (Native Americans were not interested in destroying railroads at that time.) The government agreed to Red Cloud's demands, and Red Cloud agreed to abide by the agreements in the Treaty of Fort Laramie in 1868.

The US created a new Indian agency called Red Cloud Agency. The agency would be moved and eventually turned into a reservation. After an 1870 trip to Washington, DC, Red Cloud had many of his fears confirmed when he saw the technology and numbers of European-Americans. He agreed to take his people to the Sioux reservation but continued to fight for his people. When gold was found in the sacred Black Hills, he fought to keep white miners out of the area. He did not participate in the Sioux War of 1876-1877, led by his colleague Crazy Horse and another Lakota leader named Sitting Bull. Red Cloud died in 1909, outliving many of those he fought with and against.

Chapter 14: The Battle of the Little Bighorn and Wounded Knee

The Battle of the Little Bighorn

George Armstrong Custer was born in 1839 in Ohio. After attending normal school, he applied for West Point and was accepted. He graduated last of his class of 34 in 1861 and chose his command to be in the cavalry. If his last-place finish at West Point caused him any concern, there is no evidence. Just as he entered the US Army, the Civil War began, and he quickly showed himself to be energetic and ambitious. In a short amount of time, he was promoted to brigadier general of volunteers and led the Michigan Cavalry Brigade to many victories. He made a name for himself by leading from the front, like commanders in ancient times, putting himself in the same danger he asked his men to enter. They loved him for it. He became known for his knack for avoiding serious injury; some called it the "Custer Luck." He eventually reached the level of major general.

When the Civil War ended, the volunteer army was demobilized, and Custer assumed his original rank of captain. In 1866, he became lieutenant colonel of the 7th Cavalry Regiment. He was involved in skirmishes with Native Americans, for which he was court-martialed. He was also found guilty of absence from command without leave, conduct prejudicial to military discipline, and ordering deserters shot without a trial. Once again, if these crimes seriously concerned him, it isn't known. It did not overly concern his superiors, who had him reinstated after a brief interval.

Chief Sitting Bull of the Lakota.
https://en.wikipedia.org/wiki/File:Sitting_Bull_by_D_F_Barry_ca_1883_Dakota_Territory.jpg

Custer once again began fighting in the Yellowstone area with Lakota and Cheyenne. This was the first but not the last time he would face warriors led by Sitting Bull, Crazy Horse, and Chief Gall. His regiment was tasked with protecting a survey crew from the Northern Pacific Railroad. Next, the 7th was called on to locate a suitable place for a fort in the Black Hills region. Custer had two miners brought along on the expedition, and those miners verified the rumors that there were, in fact, gold deposits in the Black Hills area. Word of the discovery quickly spread. The US government grew interested in removing the Native Americans in the Black Hills and relocating them to reservations in Indian Territory.

In 1875, the commissioner of Indian Affairs made it known that all Lakota and Cheyenne must leave the Black Hills and go to the Great Sioux Reservation by January 31, 1876, or they would be considered "hostiles." The Lakota and Cheyenne ignored the threat. So, in 1876, Gen. Philip Sheridan developed a strategy to force them to the reservation. Col. John Gibbon, with 450 men, would leave Fort Ellis in March, as would Gen. George Crook, with 1,000 men from Fort Fetterman.

Additionally, Gen. Alfred Terry would take 879 men and march out from Fort Abraham Lincoln; a large part of this contingent was the 7th Cavalry led by Lt. Col. George Custer. The idea was that one of these forces would engage what was believed to be 800 to 1,500 warriors. They were unaware that all the Lakota and Cheyenne in the area had come together for spring hunting and the early summer Sun Dance. While gathered in their temporary village, Chief Sitting Bull had a vision of soldiers falling upside down into the village. He believed it was a sign of a great victory to come.

On June 22, Gen. Alfred Terry sent Custer and the 7th to make a flanking move from the south and east of where they believed the Native Americans to be. Custer would be the hammer, while Terry would lead the anvil that would stop the enemy's escape. On June 24, Crow and Arikara scouts informed Custer of a village on the Little Bighorn River. Custer advanced towards the location, and on June 25, he was safely in the Wolf Mountains, waiting for the right moment to attack. However, the scouts soon told him the village had been discovered their presence. In the village, there was much talk of soldiers hiding in the Wolf Mountains, but many disregarded it because they couldn't imagine soldiers attacking them when they were gathered in such large numbers. There were about 8,000 people in the village, with as many as 2,500 warriors.

Custer, fearing that the element of surprise had been lost, ordered his men to advance. He broke his regiment into four groups: the pack train, a group under the command of Capt. Frederick Benteen, another under Maj. Marcus Reno, and the last 210 men under Custer's command. They each approached the village and immediately met heavy resistance. While the warriors were momentarily surprised, they quickly regained themselves and opened fire on the various small bands of cavalry. Men were caught in ditches, surrounded by Lakota and Cheyenne, and shot to pieces. Custer's fate will never be completely known, but archaeologists have pieced together the last moments of his command. In the end, the quick actions of the warriors, superior numbers, and firepower won the day. Of the 210 men under Custer's command, none survived. Others escaped and limped to meet General Terry, who would be the first to discover the aftermath of the Battle of the Little Bighorn.

It was a glorious victory for the Lakota and Cheyenne, but as is often the case, it was short-lived. "Custer's Last Stand" became a rallying cry all over America, encouraging the army to invest more manpower and firepower into removing the Native Americans. Within a year of the battle, every "hostile" had surrendered and moved to the Sioux Reservation, and the US government had taken the Black Hills without any compensation or treaty with the Lakota or Cheyenne.

Wounded Knee

The Ghost Dance, which blended messianic Christian ideas with traditional native beliefs, began with a vision by a Paiute Native American named Wovoka. It foretold that a messiah would come to save the Native Americans, European-Americans would vanish from the North American continent, the great numbers of bison would return to the plains, and the living and dead would be reunited. This would all come to pass as long as Native Americans returned to traditional ways and performed the Ghost Dance correctly. This belief spread through Native American communities, reaching the Pine Ridge Reservation in South Dakota by 1890.

Daniel F. Royer had recently become the agent at Pine Ridge. Royer was an interesting pick because he was deeply afraid of Native Americans and was convinced that they would massacre all the whites at Pine Ridge at any moment. Royer became even more concerned when the Ghost Dance reached the reservation. He believed that the Oglala Lakota performing the Ghost Dance were performing a war dance that indicated eventual bloodshed. He sent many distressing reports to Washington, DC, asking for assistance. In November of 1890, President Benjamin Harrison sent troops to the area. Reporters who traveled with the soldiers described the action as an attempt to address the crisis at Pine Ridge. However, when the soldiers and reporters arrived, there was no real crisis. The Native Americans seemed peaceful and were simply performing the Ghost Dance without any sign of aggression towards whites.

Still, rumors began to fly, and the press picked up on any scrap of information that could add fuel to the flames. With Royer still concerned about an attack and the press adding to the now-building tension, the situation quickly turned into a crisis without any foundation. Royer banned the Ghost Dance from Pine Ridge, and the Lakota were once again classified as "hostile" or "friendly." All of the Ghost Dancers were judged to be hostile and so were treated harshly. Then, on December 15, Ghost Dancer and Lakota Chief Sitting Bull was killed by an Indian agency policeman while he was being arrested on vague charges. The shock of Sitting Bull's murder sent ripples through all the reservations—especially the Lakota reservations. One such reservation was the Cheyenne River

Reservation. There the Miniconjou Lakota, led by Big Foot, were getting very nervous about their safety. The military was concerned that Big Foot would lead his people out of the reservation.

Military leaders asked a man named John Dunn to tell Big Foot that his people should stay on the reservation. For reasons unknown, Dunn instead told the Miniconjou that the military was coming to arrest the men of their tribe and deport them to an island in the Atlantic Ocean. So, he suggested, they should leave and go to Pine Ridge Reservation. On December 23, Big Foot took Dunn's advice and led his people out of the Cheyenne River Reservation at night towards the Badlands. The US Army, primarily the 7th Cavalry Regiment, pursued them for five days. Finally, on December 28, they caught up to Big Foot's band and confined them to a camp near Wounded Knee Creek.

The next day, Col. James Forsyth told them they had to give up their firearms and move to a new camp. The Miniconjou took this to mean they would be marched to Indian Territory, away from their ancestral homes, which they found unacceptable. Some began to perform the Ghost Dance, which the soldiers found threatening. A Lakota named Black Coyote refused to give up his gun. A soldier tried to wrestle it from him, and the gun went off. The soldiers gathered there immediately began firing into the Lakota crowd; soon, this included cannons with exploding rounds. The Miniconjou tried to flee but were gunned down. Some were able to get to their guns and return fire, but the soldiers rode them down. Bodies were found as far as three miles from the campsite.

Aftermath of Wounded Knee Massacre.
https://en.wikipedia.org/wiki/File:Wounded_Knee_aftermath5.jpg

When the dust settled, twenty-five soldiers had been killed, while 250 to 300 Lakota men, women, and children had been killed. The papers called it the Battle of Wounded Knee, but today it has been appropriately recognized as a massacre. Colonel Forsythe was investigated but eventually found not guilty. The Secretary of War at the time, Redfield Proctor, concluded that he believed many of the Lakota women and children had been killed, at first, by the Lakota warriors. For Native Americans, especially those with Lakota heritage, the Wounded Knee Massacre came to symbolize US government's disregard for their lives. From the first days of the country's formation, the US military and politicians had told Native Americans that they would protect the tribes as long as they were peaceful. Here was a group of Native Americans—lied to, scared, confused, trying to find safety—that had been harassed and then gunned down for no apparent reason. They were committing no crime, and they weren't acting hostile or threatening, yet they were treated as criminals and killed without provocation. Wounded Knee will certainly always remain in the Native American mind, not just as a tragedy but as a warning.

SECTION FOUR:
FREEDOM AT WHAT COST?

Chapter 15: The Freedmen of the Five Tribes

Native Americans practiced a form of slavery before the arrival of European colonists. In North America, slaves were typically men and women from enemy tribes or villages captured during war. These slaves were often adopted into the tribe and were eventually given their freedom. They were certainly not considered a piece of property. However, during the late 18th century when the British and Americans were interacting with the tribes of the Southeast, Native Americans there were introduced to chattel slavery. At first, they themselves were taken to be slaves, or they captured people from other tribes and traded them for goods. Eventually, however, to assimilate with white Americans, the people of the Five Civilized Tribes adopted the practice of owning Black slaves in the same manner as white plantation owners. One of the factors that made the Cherokee, Chickasaw, Choctaw, Muscogee Creek, and Seminole "civilized" was that they practiced chattel slavery. Still, by the 1830s and 1840s, this was not enough for Americans to consider Native Americans equals. And so, they and their slaves were forced on the Trail of Tears to Indian Territory west of Arkansas. Slavery continued on the reservations until the Civil War.

As previously discussed, some Native American leaders desired to stay neutral during the Civil War, but wealthy slaveholders in the reservations pushed for the five tribes to support the Confederacy—largely because they feared a Union victory would mean the end of slavery. Some Native

Americans favored the South because the Confederate diplomats promised greater respect for Native American rights. By October 1861, all five tribes had signed treaties with the Confederacy. Still, many people in the five tribes supported the Union. Some of these were anti-slavery, while others were angered by the coercion that seemed to be behind the treaties made with the South. Among the Cherokee, there was the Keetoowah Society, a secret abolitionist organization. The Muscogee and Seminole allowed escaped slaves, also known as freedom seekers, to stay in their reservations. Those who sided with the Union often fled the reservations. Native American units on both sides fought for control of Indian Territory during the course of the war. Finally, on June 23, 1865, Cherokee Brig. Gen. Stand Waite surrendered to Union forces; he was the last Confederate general to surrender in the entire war.

Interestingly enough, the Cherokee had already freed their slaves in accordance with President Lincoln's Emancipation Proclamation of 1863. After the end of the Civil War, the US government declared that all treaties with the five tribes were null and void. In 1866, a new set of treaties were established for each of the tribes. The main feature in all the treaties was the abolition of slavery in Indian Territory. This freed approximately 7,000 enslaved persons. It was up to the tribes to decide how they would incorporate these freedmen. The Muscogee Creek and Seminole immediately gave the freedmen in their reservations full citizenship and privileges. Previously enslaved people in Cherokee territory were entitled to full citizenship only if they were living within the reservation when the treaty was signed. If they had left, as many had due to the fighting, they needed to return within six months after the treaty's signing to be eligible. Many former slaves who had fled Cherokee territory returned too late and were not given their citizenship rights. This resulted in many families with both citizen members and those who were considered "intruders" and could not vote. The Cherokee asked the federal government to help them eject these "intruders."

The Choctaw and Chickasaw enacted "Black Codes" that determined wages for former slaves and required freedmen to get jobs or go to jail. They did not allow any slaves that left their territory to return, and freed slaves still did not have the right to vote or hold office, even though the 1866 treaties required that they be given those rights. The Choctaw and Chickasaw resorted to violence to drive freed slaves out of their territory. Much of the tension was centered around the Leased District, part of Choctaw and Chickasaw land between the 98th and 100th meridian and the Canadian River and Red River in Oklahoma. In 1855, the US government leased this land from the Choctaw and Chickasaw for $800,000 to be used as a home for the Wichita Tribe and other tribes. However, because they supported the Confederacy, the Choctaw and Chickasaw were only awarded $300,000 for this land. The treaty of 1866 gave the tribes an option to adopt the freedmen in their territory and receive $300,000 or have the ex-slaves granted the money after they had been removed from Indian Territory. The majority of Choctaw and Chickasaw seem to have favored the removal of ex-slaves, but their petitions were ignored by the US. In Choctaw territory, freedmen did not become citizens until 1883 and were discouraged from voting and banned from holding office. The Choctaw were finally awarded $52,000 for their share of the Leased District. The Chickasaw, however, never gave their freedmen citizenship rights.

In the 1870 census, 68,152 people were living in Indian Territory. Of that number, 6,378 were African Americans, most of whom were ex-slaves and their descendants. Culturally, the freedmen in Indian Territory were closely linked to the Native American cultures from which they came. They spoke Native American languages and ate Native American food. However, most freemen also spoke English, which set them apart from other Native Americans.

Except for the Choctaw and Chickasaw violence of 1866, freedmen in Indian Territory were not subject to the violence and hatred their counterparts experienced in the American South. In the Cherokee Nation, freedmen had the right to vote. In the Creek and Seminole nations, the freedmen were afforded full political representation. The situation in the Creek and Seminole nations encouraged other freedmen to migrate to their territory for the same benefits.

Freedmen were often given certain protections and assistance. They were given allotments to grow crops, and there is no indication they were singled out to get the lowest-producing land. The Creek and Seminole gave the freedmen river lots perfect for growing cotton. Many Cherokee freedmen, like those in Creek and Seminole land, became prosperous entrepreneurs with growing businesses.

Oil was eventually discovered in the Cherokee Nation, and by 1890, Native Americans were a minority in their own land. Of the 178,097 people in Oklahoma Territory, about 50,000 were Native American, 18,000 were African American, and almost 110,000 were white.

Most African Americans were from other states and not descendants of Native American freedmen. This greatly changed the race relations in Indian Territory. Many of the Native American freedmen disliked the new influx of African Americans, whom they called "state Negroes." The increase in African Americans in Indian Territory led to a strong reaction by Native Americans. In 1891, the Choctaw passed a law that anyone employing African American servants would be fined $50 and tried to push all the African Americans out of their land. Even the Creek, known for their liberal attitude towards race, received protests when African American troops were stationed in their territory. The Indian agent of 1898 reported that the Creek would not sell or rent land to any African Americans and were actively trying to push them out of their land.

In 1893 came the Dawes Commission, which was designed to terminate the separate agreements with the Five Civilized Tribes and give individual allotments, 160 acres, to every member of the tribes. In 1896, the commission was directed to create rolls (lists) of all citizens, Native American and freemen, for each tribe. Using these, the US government would determine Native American citizenship and give out land accordingly. The tribes were no longer allowed to determine who was a member and who was not. Under the Dawes Rolls, freedmen were finally recognized as citizens in the Chickasaw tribe and accounted for 36 percent of the tribe. Many Native Americans were, understandably, bitter about the situation. They felt that many outsiders were presenting false proof to get on the rolls, especially freedmen. In truth, some African Americans were convinced by land speculators to provide dubious claims. The speculators would then buy the land cheaply once the claim was approved.

In 1907, Indian Territory and Oklahoma Territory were combined and brought into the Union as the state of Oklahoma. The promises of sovereignty and any small claims of autonomy from 1830 were officially taken away. The vast majority of the population of Oklahoma was white. They instituted segregation, recognizing Native Americans as white. African Americans did not have the right to vote. The territory once controlled by Native Americans and a haven for African Americans was now controlled by white supremacy. While Native Americans were considered white for certain legislation, they were not accepted as equals in white communities.

Chapter 16: Legacy and Historiography

Flag of the American Indian Movement.
Tripodero, CC0, via Wikimedia Commons;
https://commons.wikimedia.org/wiki/File:Flag_of_the_American_Indian_Movement_V2.svg

Much of the history of Native Americans, including the Five Tribes, from 1907 to the present has been a struggle for recognition and equal rights. For instance, the Wounded Knee Occupation of 1973 was a protest against corruption within tribal governments and the failure of the US government to adhere to previously signed treaties. This particular protest involved Oglala Lakota and members of the American Indian Movement who sought to address the myriad of issues facing Native Americans in modern times, from lack of education funds to police brutality and poverty. The Federal Bureau of Investigation (FBI) and US Marshals were called in, and a seventy-one-day siege resulted in two activists being killed and two more going missing, including civil rights leader Ray Robinson. An FBI agent was paralyzed, and several others were injured. In 2014, the FBI released that Robinson had been killed, perhaps due to a disagreement with tribal leaders.

The Wounded Knee Occupation was part of a much longer story, of course. In 1956, the Indian Relocation Act had helped Native Americans move from rural areas to cities to gain opportunities, but it also helped alienate Native Americans from their cultural roots and depopulate tribal lands. This was seen as part of the so-called Indian termination policy in the US from the 1940s to the 1960s. Critics argued that this period, which saw a large amount of federal and state legislation, was designed to terminate tribes altogether and force Native Americans to abandon their tribal identifications and become simply American citizens. In particular, they cited Public Law 280, which sought to transfer law enforcement in Indian reservations from federal control to local sheriff control in several states. This took away the power of tribes to put non-natives on trial for crimes committed on reservation land.

In 1978, the American Indian Movement organized the first Longest Walk. This was a spiritual walk across the country to raise awareness of federal activities that would negatively impact Native Americans. The walk began on Alcatraz Island in San Francisco and ended at the Washington Monument in Washington, DC, covering over 3,000 miles. That year, Congress passed the American Indian Religious Freedom Act, which protected several aspects of Native American religious practices. Another Longest Walk took place in 2008 and focused attention on protecting sacred sites, climate change, and tribal sovereignty, among other issues.

For scholars and researchers working on the history of Native Americans, significant thought must be given to the contemporary attitudes of Native Americans living in the United States. As with the narratives in African American history, historians must be aware of the modern audience and the implications of their work. The narratives of the Five Civilized Tribes cannot be told without context and a greater understanding of the Native American experience. One might conclude that the Cherokee tribe, for instance, was a tribal descendant of the Mississippian Culture, but one should remember that according to Cherokee oral tradition, the tribe has existed from time immemorial. It is not just historians that tell the Cherokee story; they tell the story themselves. Today you can visit www.cherokee.org and read their account of their history, as well as current news on their nation and the activities of their tribe. The Muscogee (Creek) Nation also operates a website at www.muscogeenation.com. The site has little in the way of history but is more focused on the present and providing news and resources to members of the Muscogee tribe. Their history is a living history, being written today in quarterly reports and the passing of important bills.

Historians must be willing to tell the complete story of the Five Tribes. In the past, historians have wanted to present Native Americans as savages and place the blame for their circumstances squarely on their own shoulders. These early American historians did not want to cast the United States government in an unflattering light. Then historians began to reveal the details of incidents like the Sand Creek and Wounded Knee massacres and the breaking of treaties by the federal government. Every US history textbook included at least some information on the Trail of Tears. However, these historians tended to gloss over slavery within the Five Tribes and would not mention that it was not only Native Americans but also enslaved people who walked the Trail of Tears.

Modern historians attempt to provide a more holistic view of the narratives of Native Americans. In their efforts, they must confront the reality that many Native Americans copied American attitudes about race and gender to be viewed as equals with white Americans. Some Native Americans fought the encroachment of Americans and the British before them; others allied themselves with the Americans and fought other tribes or even members of their own tribe they disagreed with. Native Americans were undoubtedly treated horribly in many instances, and almost all whites assumed they were of an inferior race. However, it is just as close-minded to think of Native Americans as an entirely cohesive group. They were and are a population of complicated people with a wide array of motives and interests, no different from any other society—except, perhaps, their long history of having their land and culture taken by persuasion and force with no regard to their rights. This truth is shared by every tribe and group of Native Americans across the continent and has led them to align themselves with other indigenous people treated in a similar fashion, such as the native populations of Hawaii and the Māori people of New Zealand.

Conclusion

The legacy of the Native Americans is a colorful and sometimes somber tapestry that is essential to the understanding of the American experience. The names of many states, towns, universities, and rivers are derived from Native American names. The story of the American frontier is almost always the story of the struggle between Native Americans who lived and used the land and the settlers who wanted the land. However, American history has a habit of erasing the presence of Native Americans. Even the idea of the frontier and the unclaimed wilderness that the expanding United States bordered belies the fact that the wilderness was not all that wild and belonged to people who hunted and farmed the land. Early British colonists would walk through fields they considered overgrown, not realizing they were actually planted fields of corn, bean, and squash—just not planted in clearly defined rows as they were used to. Before the arrival of Europeans, Native Americans did not have metal axes, so they cleared their land using controlled burning. Trees were felled by burning a ring at the base. Europeans and Americans did not recognize the methods Native Americans used to maintain their land and therefore assumed they had done nothing and had no rights to their homeland.

When Native Americans have appeared in books, films, and TV, they are often portrayed as the enemy or an obstacle that must be overcome. Very rarely are they shown in the company of white Americans, fighting alongside them. History books and websites are quick to speak of the Red Sticks in the Creek War but often leave out the White Sticks who fought alongside American soldiers to defeat their quarrelsome brothers. In popular entertainment, Native Americans have often been something to fear, but in modern times they are often either something to be revered or pitied. Native Americans are often shown as inscrutable and perhaps mystical. Rarely are they portrayed as human, with foibles and dreams. Americans struggle with how to represent them because they are not simply another cultural group, but a group that white Americans have a troublesome history with.

However, recent efforts have been made to cast off the offensive names used in the past and given to sports teams, roads, and bridges, to name a few. Some Americans have recognized that certain things, like the presence of a portrait of Andrew Jackson, would be offensive to Native Americans. However, many Americans are still unaware of the complicated history of a man like Andrew Jackson in regard to Native Americans. This is why it is so important to tell the narratives of Native Americans to modern audiences. Only after seeing the larger picture can one understand the current situation. With this large-scale view in mind, it is much easier to address the contemporary world and see possible paths to a better future.

Part 2: Trail of Tears

An Enthralling Guide to the Choctaw and Chickasaw Removal, the Seminole Wars, Creek Dissolution, and Forced Relocation of the Cherokee Tribe

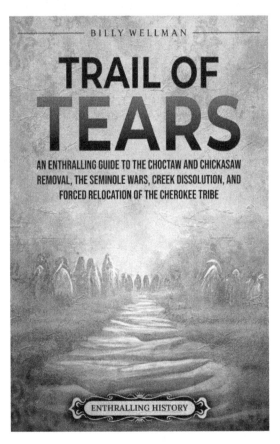

Introduction

This book tells the story of the clash between the Native American tribes that occupied the southeastern part of the United States during the 1800s and the European settlers who originally came to America to escape religious persecution. Due to their lust for land and profit, wealthy "land-jobbers" (land speculators) lured settlers westward, decimating the Native Americans who were in their path. Many treaties were made with the US government, some by tribal agreement, some by dissidents who claimed to speak for the entire tribe, and some by unscrupulous gold diggers and land-grabbers backed by corrupt politicians who wanted the land for themselves.

Often, when the settlers broke the treaties and occupied Native American land, the government overlooked these violations, hoping to avoid a conflict with the states. Given the subsequent Native American resistance to the encroachment of their lands and the response by state militias and the US military, along with the resulting massacre and displacement of many tribes, we must ask ourselves, "Was this death and destruction of the American Indian nations inevitable? Could the Native Americans and the settlers have gotten along with mutual concern for each other's well-being while sharing the land?

These are the questions that will be pondered in this book, and they revolve around the age-old question of human greed, to which there may be no answer.

Chapter 1: The Five Civilized Tribes

The Cherokee

Any story involving the Native American tribes must begin with those that have been titled the Five Civilized Tribes, those hard-working farmers and herders who mostly lived in the Southern US states. These tribes were the Cherokee, Choctaw, Muscogee (Creeks), Chickasaw, and Seminole. They earned their name because they adopted American culture more readily than other tribes, leading them to be seen as "civilized" in the eyes of the US government.

As a note, what follows is a very brief overview of the tribes, so we encourage you to learn more about their cultures. The best way to begin your research is to visit local Native American museums and cultural centers.

We will begin with the Cherokee Nation, the largest tribe in America today. They put up the fiercest resistance to the government's attempts to displace them from their ancestral homelands.

The Cherokee were an ethnic group bound together by kinship (clans) whose members spoke the Iroquoian language. They had villages in northern Georgia in the Blue Ridge Mountains and, to a lesser extent, on the Upper Savannah River. They had extensive relations, albeit not always friendly, with the Creek and the Sappony, who lived in the Piedmont area on the North Carolina-Virginia border. The Cherokee was the most populous tribe east of the Mississippi, and their clans were spread across the Carolinas, Georgia, Alabama, and Tennessee.[1]

A Cherokee nation was a confederacy of towns under a supreme war chief or a supreme peace chief. The natives in the red (war) towns were under the supreme war chief, and the natives in the white (peace) towns were ruled by, you guessed it, the supreme peace chief.

The Cherokee, like many other tribes, banded together to fight the encroachment of white settlers. However, they had a unique system of beliefs, including the Bear Dance (Yona), where they danced around a fire or pot with gourd and tortoise shell rattles.

Another thing that distinguished the Cherokee from other tribes was the fact they tended to side with the British in trade and war, which brought them into conflict with the colonies when they expanded westward. Since the colonists were encroaching on Native American land, they denied the natives access to their hunting grounds, in effect destroying the economic sustenance upon which they relied. The Cherokee were drawn into several wars by the British. For instance, they fought against the Yamasee in 1715 in South Carolina, which led to a forty-year war between the Cherokee and the Creeks.[2]

However, by 1759 the British and Cherokee were at each other's throats. Open warfare broke out since the Cherokee felt they had not been rewarded for their efforts in aiding the British against the French and other Native American tribes. During the Anglo-Cherokee War (1758–1761), each side accused the other of betrayals during the French and Indian War. The British burned villages and slaughtered the Cherokee, and the Cherokee attacked settlers.

With the Treaty of Long Island of Holston (1777), a temporary peace ensued, as the Cherokee were given Long Island in exchange for giving up their claims in east Tennessee. Eventually, the Cherokee again sided with the British against the colonists, only to be persecuted and slaughtered by Southern militias. A brave Cherokee warrior named Dragging Canoe continued the fight after numerous treaties were violated and more land was lost. For ten years after the American Revolution, Dragging Canoe led the Chickamauga Cherokees in a last-ditch effort to work with the British

---

[1] Boulware, Tyler. "Cherokee Indians." *New Georgia Encyclopedia*, 20 January 2009, https://www.georgiaencyclopedia.org/articles/history-archaeology/cherokee-indians/.

[2] Ibid.

and other Native American tribes, but the Cherokee warriors were ultimately forced to give up the fight.

The "Federal Road," the main road from southern Georgia to Knoxville, Tennessee, was the gateway to the West. In his second term, President George Washington designated this as a westward mail route, but by 1806, under the Tellico Treaty, the Cherokee were paid $1,600 to ferry travelers through Cherokee territory. In time, the settlers encroached on the Cherokee lands, thereby wiping out their hunting grounds, which eventually led to their displacement in Oklahoma.[3]

Prior to this removal, many Cherokee chiefs resisted the removal efforts, pointing to the Treaty of Hopewell (1785), which laid out the boundaries between the US and the Cherokee Confederacy. Cherokee Chief John Ross led the resistance group known as the Cherokee Triumvirate, which consisted of himself, Charles Hicks, and Major Ridge. Together, they crafted the Treaty of 1819, in which the government aided Cherokees who agreed to give up land in the Southeast for land west of the Mississippi.

The" Peace Party," those Cherokee leaders who wanted the Cherokee Nation to move to Oklahoma, went against the wishes of Chief John Ross by negotiating the Treaty of New Echota in 1835, which agreed to the removal of all Cherokee beyond the Mississippi. Those dissident Cherokees, led by Major Ridge, who had earlier sided with John Ross, would later pay the price for his fraudulent actions. His son, John Ridge, and nephew, Elias Boudinot, who also signed the treaty, would also lose their lives.

Thus, the Cherokee Nation ceased to exist as a unified body in the American Southeast due to warfare, starvation, disease, and loss of economic sustenance. After several years of disagreements with the Peace Party and the Cherokee Triumvirate, those who had not already left ultimately agreed to relocate to Oklahoma. John Ross traveled to Washington, DC, to negotiate the withdrawal of the remaining Cherokee, and the federal government provided them with two million dollars for their journey west.

---

[3] Ibid.

The Choctaw

The Choctaw originated from Mexico and western America and lived in the Mississippi River Valley along the Old Natchez Trace Forest Trail, which was the main trading route between the eastern and southern frontiers. This area, the Southeast Woodland areas of Alabama, Mississippi, and Louisiana, was the homeland of this Muskogean tribe of warriors.

Their life was centered around agriculture. The Choctaw grew corn and beans, which they traded with other tribes, the Europeans, and the Americans. They played stickball and chunky stone (*tchung-kee*), which they used to "prepare for war or as an alternative to war." In the game of chunky stone, disk-shaped stones were rolled across the ground. Then, the players threw spears to see who could get the closest.[4]

Another interesting fact about the Choctaw is that they found flat heads attractive. One of their customs was to tie a board or bag of sand to a child's head at birth to flatten the skull until it became elongated like a football.

The Choctaw were known for having a matriarchal society and their elaborate celebration of the harvest, known as the Green Corn Festival. The Choctaw diet included fish, corn, squash, deer, bear, nuts, and beans. All of these commodities were valuable trading assets.

Like the Cherokee, the Choctaw were skilled traders, warriors, and consumers, but unfortunately, they, too, met the same fate as the other tribes who were displaced. The Choctaw aligned themselves with the British in the 1700s and 1800s for trade and security connections, but in the process, they became involved in wars against other tribes. Eventually, they sided with the French to decimate the Natchez tribe.

Chief Pushmataha was the most famous Choctaw. He fought with the Americans in the War of 1812 and negotiated treaties with the US government. However, in the end, it was all in vain. The monopolistic land speculators from the Northeast began selling land parcels in the Mississippi Valley, luring settlers to the area, which caused them to clash with the Choctaw.

---

[4] "Early Choctaw History." https://www.nps.gov/natr/learn/historyculture/choctaw.htm.

Pushmataha was honored as a brigadier general of the US Army and buried in the Congressional Cemetery.

https://commons.wikimedia.org/wiki/File:Pushmataha_high_resolution.jpg

After President Andrew Jackson passed the Indian Removal Act of 1830, seventy thousand Choctaw walked the Trail of Tears, which went through Georgia, Tennessee, Mississippi, and Arkansas. The Choctaw were rounded up and placed in camps with little time for packing belongings, so they often had no blankets or shoes. The supply outposts charged high prices and were often raided by settlers. The Cherokee were better prepared, as they had doctors and supply depots along the way, but the journey to Oklahoma was still arduous. Around four thousand Cherokees and about three thousand Choctaws died along the way. It should be noted that the numbers of deaths vary wildly from source to source; we have chosen to go with the most agreed-upon numbers in this book.

Muscogee (Creek)

Like the Cherokee and the Choctaw, the Creek was also a warrior tribe, although there was more to these tribes than warfare. One of the most notable Creek leaders was Chief Menawa, meaning "The Great Warrior," who led his Red Stick fighters (those who carried red-painted war clubs) during the Battle of Horseshoe Bend (modern-day Alabama) in 1814 and in the fight against General Andrew Jackson's troops at Enitichopco Creek.

Menawa was the chief of Okfuskee and owned large herds of cattle and hogs. He traded horses and pelts with people in Pensacola but eventually became incensed by the encroachment of Creek lands in Georgia and

Alabama by the settlers. Menawa began raiding settlements and towns to steal horses, which brought him into conflict with General Jackson's forces at Horseshoe Bend.[5]

The Creek, like the Cherokee to the north and Choctaw to the east, were agricultural tribes. They cultivated corn, beans, squash, pumpkins, melons, and sweet potatoes. They also had a manufacturing company in Columbus, Georgia, where they made baskets, pottery, and colorful deerskins. The Creek also traded beeswax, hides, furs, honey, and venison.

The Creek Confederacy became splintered after Jackson defeated them at Horseshoe Bend and forced them to cede half of Alabama. Jackson's role in the Battle of Horseshoe Bend helped propel him to the presidency, where he enacted a law that moved the Southeastern tribes west of the Mississippi. An estimated 3,500 Creeks died on the Trail of Tears.[6]

The Chickasaw: Chikasha-Saya ("I am Chickasaw")

The Chickasaw had a great love of tattoos (war paint), which they believed enhanced their warrior spirit. The Chickasaw were ferocious warriors and were known as the "Spartans of the Mississippi." They participated in many battles with other tribes and against the white settlers.[7] They lived in Mississippi, Alabama, Tennessee, and Kentucky until 1832, when they were forced to move to Oklahoma.

Like the Cherokee, Choctaw, and Creek, the Chickasaw was an agricultural nation that carried out trade with the British and French, but in many ways, they were different from the other Civilized Tribes. They had a network of towns in Alabama, Kentucky, and Tennessee, and their capital was in Tishomingo, Mississippi. The Chickasaw established laws, religion, a constitution with a legislative and executive branch, and popular elections.

We are told they fought with the French against the British in the French and Indian War and that the Chickasaw Mounted Regiment ultimately aided the South in the Civil War. Following the war, they became successful farmers and ranchers while building schools, banks, and businesses in Native American territory.

---

[5] Braund, Kathryn. "Menawa." http://encyclopediaofalabama.org/article/h-3594

[6] Haveman, Christopher. "Creek Indian Removal." http://encyclopediaofalabama.org/article/h-2013.

[7] "History: Chickasaw Nation." https://www.chickasaw.net/our-nation/history.aspx

The Doaksville Treaty of 1837 sealed this semi-nomadic tribe's fate. The Chickasaw was the last of the Five Civilized Tribes forced by the US government to travel on the Trail of Tears. Between five hundred to one thousand Chickasaw died on the journey.

The Seminole

The Seminole arrived in what is now called Florida long before the Spanish. The Spanish called them *"Cimarrones,"* which means "wild ones" or "runaways" due to the Seminoles constantly eluding capture. The tribe had members across Florida, Georgia, and Alabama, and they designated themselves as unconquered people who sought freedom from conquest.[8]

The Seminoles traded with the Spanish, and in turn, the Spanish bought leather and cattle from them. The Seminoles were known for sewing, patchwork, chickee building (a type of log cabin building), and alligator wrestling. They lived in palm-thatched houses (chickees), wore ornamental clothing, celebrated the passing of the seasons, and practiced their ancestral forms of music and dance.[9]

One of their great warrior chiefs was Abiaka, a war chief of the Panther Clan. He was considered a great medicine man who became chief when others were too old or had emigrated. Abiaka, also known as Sam Jones, led his warriors deep into the swamps, where they could successfully fight the American soldiers. Abiaka was the chief of the Miccosukee (a Seminole-Creek tribe) and guided his people through the swamps during the many decades of warfare. They shadowed the American soldiers as they navigated the swamps, so the US soldiers were constantly subjected to surprise attacks. Although the swamps were rife with disease, Abiaka was knowledgeable in medicinal herbs, saving the lives of his men numerous times.[10]

Abiaka used guerrilla warfare or hit-and-run tactics to fight the American soldiers. A cook named Martha Jane stated that at a meeting with a US general in 1847, Abiaka supposedly said, "My mother died [here], my father died here, and be damned I die here too." His resistance to moving to where the white settlers wanted him to go was so strong that

---

[8] "Introduction." https://www.semtribe.com/stof/history/introduction .

[9] "Seminole History." https://dos.myflorida.com/florida-facts/florida-history/seminole-history/

[10] "Abiaka (Seminole Indian Sam Jones) - One of the Greatest Medicine Men in History." https://worldprophesy.blogspot.com/2015/01/abiaka-one-of-greatest-medicine-men-seminole.html.

he supposedly killed his sister when she thought about emigrating. He was so hateful toward the white settlers that he often threw down the money offered to him and refused to even look at them.

Due to his determination and skill as a great medicine man and leader, Abiaka was never captured, no matter how hard General Zachary Taylor, the last general who pursued him, tried. Abiaka eventually died in the swamps he loved.[11]

About five hundred Seminoles remained in Florida after the fighting, as the US grew weary of its war with the tribe since no real progress was being made. However, many Seminoles either left willingly or were forced to leave.

[11] Ibid.

Chapter 2: Sinister Origins

With this basic background on the Five Civilized Tribes, we can begin to understand the clash of civilizations that took place in America between 1810 and 1860, a clash that affected more than just five tribes. The element of greed came into play, as the white settlers desired the natives' land. Speculators trespassed on Native American lands, searching for gold, and negotiated contracts to build railroads. Swamps were drained, and canals were dug, all at the expense of the Native American tribes, who lost their hunting grounds and were forced to flee into the swamps and woodlands of North America.

It did not matter that the Native Americans were becoming Europeanized. Christianity was becoming more and more prevalent, displacing indigenous religions. Some tribes that had previously depended on hunting were now farming, and many were developing different forms of government. Meanwhile, the settlers were pushing westward at a rapid pace, bulldozing anything or anyone in their path. The wealthy speculators and the state governments, with the tacit approval of the federal government, enriched themselves in the process.

The quote that Yosemite Sam yelled to Bugs Bunny says it all: "There's gold in them thar hills!" Gold led to the encroachment of Native American lands by gold diggers and wealthy capitalists who sought land for their enterprises. Many historians cite General William Tecumseh Sherman's search for gold in California as igniting the Gold Rush, which, in turn, led to a gold rush on Native American lands from the Dakotas to California.

The clash between the Native Americans and the incoming settlers seemed inevitable, given the arrival of the Europeans and the "greed" inherent in the quest for material wealth. But how were the Native Americans treated before the Trail of Tears?

As we noted earlier, the Seminoles were in America before the Spanish, and they were probably the first to face the encroachment of their lands by the conquistadors led by Ponce de León and Hernando de Soto. However, that story is for another day. A good place to begin our tale would be with the Treaty of Hopewell in 1785, which was signed under the presidency of John Hancock, who was president of the Second Continental Congress. This treaty between the Cherokee, Choctaw, and Chickasaw and the United States government was signed in South Carolina. Under the terms of the treaty, the Native Americans gave up sections of their lands in return for protection. The treaty was soon violated by the encroaching settlers, and the tribal leaders refused to recognize the sovereignty of the United States or the states in which they lived.

A few years later, in 1791, President George Washington, like Andrew Jackson forty years later, made the "Indian problem" a top priority. He wanted a just policy, and like President Jackson, he may have been sincere in his wish for peace. However, in both cases, peace was not in the cards.[12]

Washington, who was purchasing large tracts of land, instructed the Administration of Indian Affairs to follow the "great principles of justice and humanity," but the administration soon learned the Continental Congress had already angered the Native Americans by ordering them to move west of the Mississippi. Secretary of War Henry Knox's opinion was expressed in his official report of June 15th, 1789, in which he "urged adoption of what he believed to be a just and humane policy that recognized Indian rights to the soil, rejected the principle of conquest, and compensated the Indians for lands they ceded."[13] But in a 1790 letter to Washington, he apparently changed his mind, saying, "it is incumbent on the United States to be in a position to punish all unprovoked aggressions."[14] This put the administration in a conundrum, and

---

[12] "Native Americans." https://www.mountvernon.org/george-washington/native-americans/ .

[13] "Report of Henry Knox on the Northwestern Indians." https://pages.uoregon.edu/mjdennis/courses/hist469_Knox.htm.

[14] Knox, Henry. "To George Washington from Henry Knox." https://founders.archives.gov/documents/Washington/05-04-02-0353.

Washington eventually came to believe the Native Americans would be better off if they were separated from the white settlers.

President Washington decided the constitutional power of treaty-making, which was to be carried out between the Senate and the president, should be applied to the Native Americans.

When the Shawnee, Miami, Ottawa, Chippewa, Iroquois, Fox, and Souk in the Ohio Valley decided they were giving up too much land, they began to resist removal. The president sent in five thousand troops under General "Mad" Anthony Wayne to put down the rebellion. In the Battle of Fallen Timbers (1794), the Native American confederation was destroyed. The Treaty of Greenville (1795) led to a period of peace, allowing Washington to turn his attention south to deal with the problems between Georgia and the Creek, Chickasaw, Choctaw, and Cherokee, four of the so-called "Civilized Tribes."

The Creeks disagreed with the three treaties they had signed with Georgia since they had been forced to cede twenty-three million acres (part of southern Georgia and half of Alabama). A delegation of twenty-eight chiefs traveled to New York for the negotiations, and under the Treaty of New York, they recovered some of their lands taken by Georgia. But the stipulations the Washington administration included in the treaty involved more than just peace. The treaty protected the Creeks in Georgia but also stated they should become "acculturated and civilized" while becoming part of land settlements where they would be subject to state laws.

Washington's thinking from his early experience with Native Americans led him to believe the natives should be Europeanized, as it would allow them to blend in easier with white society and overcome the prejudices they faced. As such, the treaty stipulated the Creeks should give up hunting and become "herdsmen and cultivators."

But again, as we glance into the future, George Washington had the same problem as Andrew Jackson and Martin Van Buren: an overwhelming influx of white settlers moving toward the western frontier. This is a fact that critics of the Native Americans' removal do not take into consideration when they castigate Andrew Jackson, who is often accused of genocide due to his Native American removal policies. An argument can certainly be made for blaming the settlers, the land speculators, the greedy, cutthroat railroad barons, and those who pushed for the expansion and growth of the United States to build it into an empire. Typically, though, the bulk of the blame is generally placed on President Jackson and Van Buren, the latter of which continued Jackson's policies.

Even back in 1776, Washington and Knox were afraid the Native American tribes would be annihilated by the throng of settlers, with Washington saying, "I believe scarcely anything short of a Chinese Wall, or a line of troops will restrain land jobbers and the encroachment of settlers upon the Indian territory."[15] So, if we want to talk about genocide or the sinister origins of the removal of Native Americans, we have to start with the white settlers and westward expansion. However, the doublespeak of politicians, along with the bribes they took from wealthy speculators, should not be overlooked either.

American historian Colin Calloway looks at the darker side of George Washington to sort of dull the shine of his American armor. As we said, Washington, like Jackson, opposed Native American removal and claimed he wanted to treat them humanely by allowing them to remain on their lands if they agreed to recognize the power of the state in which they resided, which, of course, forced them to deny their own sovereignty. Calloway argues against the idea that Washington knew that Native American removal was "inevitable" by stating that "Washington knew that he must build his nation on Indian land, and by war and diplomacy ... knowing that westward expansion pushed Indians out and turned tribal homelands into States." He says Washington's goals were first to acquire land and then to seek justice for the Native Americans. If they refused to sell, Washington was willing to wage war on them. Calloway says that Washington used the word "extirpate," which means "destroy." He extirpated the Iroquois, who, in turn, called him "Town Destroyer."[16]

We are told by other historians that Washington often invited Native American chiefs to dine with him at his home in Philadelphia. Calloway tells us that after one of these meetings with Mohawk Chief Joseph Brant, Brant warned other Native Americans that Washington talked with a forked tongue. "George Washington is very cunning, he will try to fool us if he can. He speaks very smooth, will tell you fair stories, and at the same time want to ruin us."

[15] Genovese, Michael A. & Landry, Alysa. *US Presidents and the Destruction of the Native American Nations (The Evolving American Presidency)*. Palgrave Macmillian, 2021.

[16] Calloway, Colin. "George Washington Lived in an Indian World, but His Biographies Have Erased Native People." https://longreads.com/2018/11/07/george-washington-lived-in-an-indian-world-but-his-biographies-have-erased-native-people.

He further noted that the Treaty of New York contained six "secret articles" that the Creek were not aware of when they signed the treaty with the US, but only two were ratified by the Senate. Less than a year later, Washington sent troops to destroy Native American villages in northwest Ohio because they refused to cede their ancestral land. Calloway summarizes his essay by saying that "Washington's decisions set precedents that are still with us. As the father of the country, he was also the father of America's tortuous, conflicted, and often hypocritical Indian policies."[17]

In 1811, General William Henry Harrison, the future US president, defeated Shawnee Chief Tecumseh and the Northwest tribes in the Battle of Tippecanoe in Indiana, dashing Tecumseh's hope for a Northwest Confederacy. After this followed the War of 1812, in which many Native American tribes fought with the British. Another future president, General Andrew Jackson, called "Sharp Knife" by the Native Americans because of his cruelty, battled the Red Stick warriors of the Creeks. Ultimately, twenty-three million acres of Creek land were confiscated.

Finally, in 1830, President Jackson sponsored the Indian Removal Act, which eventually forced the remaining tribes, including the Seminoles of Florida, who had already ceded four million acres under the treaty of Moultrie in 1823, west of the Mississippi. The Seminoles in Florida were attacked by the militias of Georgia and the US Army and were pushed farther south into the swamps. This was due to the competitive nature of their farming and because Native American tribes were using runaway slaves for their farms, which the plantations needed to cultivate their crops. The Seminoles continued to resist even after the Indian Removal Act was passed. The act ultimately resulted in the Second Seminole War (1835-1842), which was followed by the Third Seminole War of 1855, after which the Seminole population in Florida was reduced to only a few hundred.

The population explosion in the United States made westward expansion a necessity for the settlers, who were being lured by land speculators. The clash between land speculators and Native Americans occurred because the speculators viewed Native Americans as a stumbling block on the path to social and economic development. The idea of Manifest Destiny brought with it opportunities for farming, raising cattle,

---

[17] Ibid.

and logging. As such, the idea of Manifest Destiny, the idea that expansion was divinely ordained and justifiable, led to the removal of Native Americans from their ancestral homelands.

Emanuel Gottlieb Leutze, *Westward the Course of Empire Takes Its Way (mural study, US Capitol)*, 1861, oil on canvas, Smithsonian American Art Museum, Bequest of Sara Carr Upton, 1931.
https://commons.wikimedia.org/wiki/File:Westward_the_Course_of_Empire.jpg

Historically, many prominent Americans, such as President George Washington and President James Madison, advocated westward expansion. Of course, President Andrew Jackson (1829-1837), President Martin Van Buren (1837-1841), and President James Polk (1845-1849) supported the idea of Manifest Destiny, a term coined by newspaper editor John O'Sullivan around 1845.

The explosion of Europeans arriving on the East Coast, the land speculators who pushed them westward, and the gold rush all contributed to the move to push the Native American tribes out of their homelands.

Chapter 3: The Indian Removal Act 1830: Cause and Consequence

While many factors led to the removal of the Native Americans from their ancestral lands, Leonard Carlson and Mark Roberts, in their article titled "Indian Lands, Squatterism, and Slavery," tell us that the Southern slaveholders wanted more land in the west to grow cotton, while Northern manufacturers, led by the Whig Party, felt that expanding westward would be detrimental to businesses in New England. The dispute raged in Congress.

Meanwhile, President Andrew Jackson considered the Indian Removal Act. Squatters had settled on Native American lands and demanded to be allowed to buy the land they occupied at a low cost. Georgia, which had a large Cherokee population, demanded the tribes that had a claim to Georgian lands be removed to the west to preserve their culture and prevent their annihilation at the hands of the settlers and state militias.[18]

The Indian Removal Act gave President Jackson the authority to exchange lands west of the Mississippi for lands the Native Americans were living on within state borders. In the late 1830s, the government began to forcibly move the Cherokees and other tribes west via what came to be known as the Trail of Tears.

---

[18] Carlson, Leonard A., and Mark A. Roberts. "Indian Lands, Squatterism, and Slavery: Economic Interests and the Passage of the Indian Removal Act of 1830." *Explorations in Economic History* 43.3 (2006): 486-504. Web. www.sciencedirect.com.ezproxy.liberty.edu.

There were some people who were against the Indian Removal Act, including Congressman Davey Crockett, who declared his vote against it would "not make me ashamed in the day of judgement." 19 Christian Missionary and newspaper publisher Jerimiah Evarts used his newspaper to oppose the act. Cherokee Chief John Ross traveled many times to Washington, DC, to argue against it as well.

As a boy, Davey Crockett grew up in the wild frontier of present-day eastern Tennessee. After several skirmishes with schoolmates and reprimands by his father, the strong-willed boy ran away from home at the age of fourteen, working as a hatmaker and a cattle driver. In 1813, he joined the Tennessee militia in the fight against the Red Stick faction of the Creeks. The Red Sticks fought other Creeks and the US government, as they were vehemently opposed to becoming assimilated by the Americans. They had carried out a massacre at Fort Mims, Alabama, where hundreds of civilians were killed or captured. During the Creek War, Crockett was a scout and a game hunter but was with General Andrew Jackson when the latter massacred over two hundred Red Sticks at the Creek settlement of Tallahatchie.

Davy Crockett was elected to Congress in 1827 after a bout in the state legislature, and he used his sharp tongue to oppose Jackson's Indian Removal Act in 1830, which he voted against. In an 1834 letter, he lambasted Jackson's forced removal of the Cherokee to Oklahoma and lamented the notion that Vice President Martin Van Buren would carry out Jackson's Native American policies. Crockett threatened to move to the "wilds of Texas" if Van Buren was elected. Due to Crockett's angry opposition to Jackson's Native American policies, he was voted out of office in 1835. Angry at his loss, he uttered his famous statement, "You may all go to hell, but I will go to Texas." And that is what he did, eventually dying during the Battle of the Alamo in 1836.

In spite of vehement opposition across the country, the vote in Congress was 102 to 97, with the Senate concurring. Almost all of the Five Civilized Tribes were pressured to move west. Not everyone went along peacefully, as they did not want to leave their home. Consequently, the state militias and the government responded with military force. Forty-six thousand Native Americans were forcibly removed from their homes.

---

[19] "Davy Crockett on the Removal of the Cherokees, 1834." https://www.gilderlehrman.org/history-resources/spotlight-primary-source/davy-crockett-removal-cherokees-1834.

Thousands died of disease and starvation.20

As the violence continued, many Americans who originally opposed relocation and favored assimilation came to agree with those who supported it, not just for economic reasons but also for humanitarian ones. Abolitionists, ministers, Quakers, Baptists, Methodists, and other Christians argued that Native Americans should be moved west to preserve their culture and ensure they wouldn't be exterminated by the settlers.

A year before the Indian Removal Act was passed (1829), during the contentious congressional debate over the act, a playwright named John August Stone wrote *Metamora or The Last of the Wampanoags*, a play that portrayed the conflict between the Puritans and the Wampanoags in the 1600s. It features a Wampanoag named Metamora as a scorned and violent "savage" who declares war against the English settlers. In the end, he kills his wife to protect her from the white invaders, after which the Wampanoags are slaughtered by the settlers. (In reality, the Wampanoags were decimated by smallpox and conflicts in the 1600s. Their numbers were at around seven thousand in 1610 but dipped to around four hundred only seventeen years later.)

Historians debate whether this play, which was popular in New England, added fuel to the fire in the debate to displace the Native Americans, especially since the story resonated with what was going on at the time. President Jackson signed the Indian Removal Act into law only a year after the play came out. Others contend that Stone was taking advantage of the climate at the time and used romantic ideals to create a popular work.

Nevertheless, most scholars recognize the importance of *Metamora*, such as historian Donald B. Grose in his article "Edwin Forest, 'Metamora,' and the Indian Removal Act of 1830." The play was released at a critical time in American history and portrayed a noble Native American caught up in the battle against white settlers encroaching on Native American land. Grose writes that it was a struggle forced upon the Native Americans by the War of 1812, which "brought on powerful nationalism and egalitarianism in the United States." The play displays "the sentiment for removal and the final solution; the removal of the

---

20 "May 28, 1830 CE: Indian Removal Act."
https://education.nationalgeographic.org/resource/indian-removal-act.

Native Americans to prevent their annihilation."[21]

The play was written for a contest that Edwin Forrest, an actor, had created to find a play based on a Native American character. Stone won the prize money. Forrest based his interpretation of the character on a Choctaw named Pushmataha, whom he had met years before. Stone based the character on King Philip or Chief Metacom, who fought against the English in King Philip's War.

Edwin Forrest as Metamora in 1829.
Internet Book Archives Images, no restrictions.
https://commons.wikimedia.org/wiki/File:The_autobiography_of_Joseph_Jefferson_(1890)_(14778_655621).jpg

Metamora played in theaters around the nation and reflected the ambivalence of many concerning Native American removal, as well as the struggle between northeastern humanitarians who favored assimilation and federal and state officials who felt it better to separate the Native

---

[21] Grose, B. Donald. "Edwin Forrest, 'Metamora,' and the Indian Removal Act of 1830." *Theatre Journal*, vol. 37, no. 2, 1985, pp. 181-91. *JSTOR*, https://doi.org/10.2307/3207064. Accessed 18 Sep. 2022.

Americans and the white man.

Grose puts the play in context by stating the "timeliness of the script about contemporary white-Indian affairs cannot be disallowed, for the play and Forrest were caught up in twenty years of white expansion at the expense of the Indian's lands and rights." The protagonist in the play, Metamora, "sees heroic immortality in defeat: 'We are destroyed—now vanquished; we are no more, yet we are forever.'" Grose states the play portrays all the noble characteristics of the "savage," as well as the opposing traits of the "red devil."[22]

With its foundation in Renaissance primitivism, the stereotype of the noble savage exemplified the Native American as a person of physical beauty and natural grace, filled with an intuitive knowledge of nature and its secrets. The noble savage was elegant of speech, stoic, and loyal to friends, relatives, and loved ones. When this stereotype was brought into conflict with the other version of Native Americans, the "red devil," those who only sought out violence and the destruction of the white civilization, people were uncertain how to balance the two sides of the coin. To most, three methods were possible: willing victimization, acculturation, and extermination.

And therein lies the crux of the complex struggle between the Native Americans and white settlers that took place in the United States between 1830 and 1850, although it had started well before. The situation was more complex than most realize, and *Metamora* is a good example of the way Native Americans were shown. The play shows "the Indian who via acculturation ... rejects Indianness and becomes a white ... but is unwilling to acknowledge his inferiority ad later becomes a diabolical savage, the red devil." Grose tells us the stereotype also fulfills the European conceptualization of the wild man of folklore. "His savagery grew as much as out of his failure to be white as of out of his deeds, for the red devil has the opportunity to be a white and rejects it with force."[23]

Finally, Grose notes that *Metamora* fits in with the idea of Manifest Destiny and that it portrays all the racial concepts of the Native Americans at the time: nomadic, violent, treacherous, sadistic, and cowardly, allowing audiences in the 19th century to cheer Metamora on as a noble savage while at the same time making them look forward to his destruction.

---

[22] Ibid.

[23] Ibid.

In her article, "The Assimilation, Removal, and Elimination of American Indians," Jessica Keating of Notre Dame University further expands on the idea of assimilation, an idea she says was developed out of the Enlightenment movement of the 18th century. She agrees with Grose that it was related to the notion of Manifest Destiny, the belief that America had the divine right to progress and expand westward. But the major obstacle to expansion was the Native American tribes that were occupying and blocking the lands needed for that progress. And as resistance continued, the government passed the Indian Removal Act. Over the next few decades, the Native Americans were forcibly removed to reservations in Oklahoma.[24]

[24] Keating, Jessica. "The Assimilation, Removal, and Elimination of American Indians." *The McGraph Institute for Church Life*, (2020). https://mcgrath.nd.edu/assets/390540/expert_guide_on_the_assimilation_removal_and_elimination_of_native_americans.pdf.

Chapter 4: Seminole Resistance: This Means War

With Florida being handed over to Spain in 1783 under the Treaty of Paris, white settlers began emigrating to Florida to take advantage of the land grants the Spanish government was offering. However, this land was occupied by the Seminoles, who attacked the settlers. The problem was further exacerbated by the fact that escaped slaves sought refuge in Florida, as it was not yet part of the United States. They were being pursued by militias from Georgia that sought to capture runaway slaves while also seeking land and cattle.

In 1816, US soldiers attacked and destroyed a garrison that housed escaped slaves, killing 270 people. The Seminoles retaliated by attacking settlements along the Florida-Georgia border. The First Seminole War then broke out in 1817 after General Andrew Jackson and his forces destroyed the Seminole village of Fowltown. The Seminoles retaliated by attacking Fort Scott, killing forty-three men, women, and children. Jackson continued his attacks on Seminole villages along the Suwannee River, capturing St. Marks, a Spanish military post, and the Spanish town of Pensacola.

At this point, Spain realized that Florida was a burden. The Spanish knew they could no longer protect their settlements and signed the Transcontinental Treaty (also known as the Adams-Onís Treaty) in 1819, under which they ceded Florida to the US. The US government controlled the eastern part of the territory and two years later laid claim to West

Florida, which had also been ceded under the treaty.

The Treaty of Moultrie Creek, which was signed in 1823 by the Seminoles and the US, stated the Seminoles would be given financial aid and a reservation of four million acres in Central Florida if they agreed to capture and return escaped slaves and cede all claims to Florida. But by this time, the animosity between the Seminoles, who were attacking the settlers along the Georgia-Florida border, the Georgia militias, which were raiding Native American territories to retrieve runaway slaves, and the US military led by Andrew Jackson, which was attacking and burning Native American villages, was heating up. The treaty was ultimately violated by all sides.[25]

The Second Seminole War (1835–1842) began when an influential Seminole warrior named Osceola murdered an Indian agent named Wiley Thompson (he was originally from Virginia but served in the Georgia Senate). Osceola was named Billy Powell upon his birth. As an infant, he lived in Alabama with his Muscogee mother. His father was most likely a Scotsman named William Powell. Billy and his mother moved to Florida when he was a child. His family and other Creeks joined the Seminoles. As the years passed, the encroachment of white settlers continued to grow worse. After the Treaty of Moultrie Creek, many Seminoles, including Osceola (who got his name after joining the Seminoles), moved deeper into the unknown territories of Florida.

Together with other Seminole chiefs, such as Alligator, Jumper, Coacoochee, and Halleck-Tustennuggee, many Seminole warriors fought against the US military until their numbers began to decline. Many were killed, captured, or forcibly moved westward. In 1835, the Seminoles intensified the conflict by massacring a little over one hundred soldiers in an ambush near president-day Ocala. This was known as the Dade massacre, named after General Francis Dade, who led his soldiers through the swamps into an ambush. The Seminoles were hidden on higher ground, and General Dade was the first one killed in the battle.

Osceola and Coacooche were captured in 1837 when General Jesup tricked the Seminoles under a false flag of truce. A 1988 article in the South Florida *Sun Sentinel* says that Chief Osceola was taken on the SS *Poinsett* to a prison at Fort Moultrie, South Carolina, where he died. His

[25] Pauls, Elizabeth Prine. "Trail of Tears." Encyclopedia Britannica, 28 Mar. 2022, https://www.britannica.com/event/Trail-of-Tears. Accessed 24 August 2022.

doctor, Frederick Weedon, severed his head and took it home as a souvenir. But even with the capture and death of Chief Osceola, the Seminoles continued to resist.[26]

The Third Seminole War (1855-1858) was led by a Seminole chief named Holata Micco, who was called Billy Bowlegs by the white settlers and military. Legend says he became bowlegged from his love of riding Spanish horses. Holata Micco, which means "Alligator Chief," was the last remaining established Seminole chief to lead the resistance against white encroachment.[27] He led a band of two hundred warriors and eluded capture to the end.[28]

Though Holata Micco had signed the Treaty of Payne's Landing in 1832, which required all Seminoles to move west of the Mississippi, he refused to leave Florida, saying that he was born there and that he would die there. After the treaty, Holata Micco and his family lived in peace until surveyors and engineers destroyed his banana trees. To him, it was clear the settlers would not stop and that violence was the only answer. He waged a guerrilla war against the US Army, which, in turn, attacked Seminole villages and tracked warriors with bloodhounds.

Three thousand Seminoles had already been deported via boat from New Orleans, and the pressure was intensifying to remove the rest of them to Oklahoma. Desperate to subdue the Alligator Chief, the government sent Chief Wild Cat of the Western Seminoles to urge the defiant Bowlegs to relocate to Indian Territory. Bowlegs was offered ten thousand dollars and one thousand dollars each for his chiefs. He did not agree at first, but after his camp was destroyed in 1857, he bowed to the inevitable and changed his mind several months later.

In 1858, Bowlegs and nearly two hundred other Seminoles finally surrendered. That December, he returned to convince the last of the Seminoles to move west. The vast majority of Seminoles did not walk the Trail of Tears but were taken by boat from New Orleans to the west.

In 1859, Holata Micco (Billy Bowlegs) arrived in the territory of Arkansas with his two wives, one son, five daughters, and fifty slaves. Freed

---

[26] McIver, Stuart. "Bring Me the Head of Osceola." *Sun Sentinel.* https://www.sun-sentinel.com/news/fl-xpm-1988-01-31-8801070155-story.html.

[27] "Third Seminole War." https://www.u-s-history.com/pages/h1156.html

[28] African American Registry (AAREG), "Billy Bowlegs, Seminole Chief." https://osceolahistory.org/billy-bowlegs-iii-ahead-of-his-time/.

blacks lived in Seminole communities and served as advisors, hunters, warriors, and interpreters. But as part of the process of assimilation into American-European culture, the Five Civilized Tribes adopted slavery. In most cases, they were forced to give up their slaves when they were deported, but Bowlegs was allowed to keep his slaves.

After the forcible removal of Bowlegs and his family, there were still a couple of hundred Seminoles who refused to leave Florida. They lived in isolation until the late 1920s.

Chapter 5: Manifest Destiny: Jackson, Van Buren, and the Treaty of New Echota

Andrew Jackson, the future military hero and popular Democratic president, started his climb to the top at the age of thirteen when he was arrested in 1781 by the British for refusing to polish a British officer's boots. As time went on, his mother died from cholera while tending to wounded soldiers in the War of 1812. Meanwhile, his hatred of the British intensified. Jackson became a lawyer and moved from the South Carolina-Georgia border to Tennessee, where he became a wealthy landowner. He was elected to the House of Representatives, then the Senate, and, for a while, he was a judge. His popularity led to his appointment as major general of the Tennessee Militia. Jackson fought in the war against the British in 1812, where he won the Battle of New Orleans, ironically with the help of Choctaw warriors.[29]

In 1814, with about three thousand US soldiers and around six hundred Native American allies, Jackson fought the Red Stick faction of the Creeks, those who carried red-painted wooden clubs, a few months after they massacred settlers at Fort Mims, Alabama. The Creeks themselves were divided, which is what led to the Creek War to begin

---

[29] Biography.com Editors. "Andrew Jackson Biography." *A&E Networks.* (2017). https://www.biography.com/us-president/andrew-jackson.

with. The Red Sticks, led by Peter McQueen and William Weatherford, wanted to unite all the tribes in a war against the US, but the White Sticks under Big Warrior wanted peace.

The Creek War morphed into something larger as time passed, with the Red Sticks attacking white settlements. To put down this rebellion, the US sided with the White Stick warriors. The war culminated in the Battle of Horseshoe Bend, in which eight hundred Red Stick warriors were killed. The US government confiscated twenty-three million acres from the Creeks in Alabama and Georgia, even though many Creeks had fought against or were opposed to the Red Sticks.[30]

After Jackson's victory at New Orleans, his men nicknamed him "Old Hickory" for his toughness, and Jackson proved this nickname when he and his troops marched into Florida, which was still Spanish territory, and defeated the Seminoles at St. Marks and Pensacola in 1818. This essentially gave him control of the western part of Florida. In the 1819 Adams-Onís Treaty, Spain officially ceded the territory of Florida to the United States.

After reigning as territorial governor for two months, Jackson returned to Tennessee to begin his political career. In 1824, Senator Jackson was urged to run for the presidency, which would be the start of his war against what John Tyler called the "monied monopoly," i.e., the land speculators and their cronies in Congress who wanted a US central bank. They would profit from this venture since the bank could provide loans to them.

According to Thomas DiLorenzo, in his book *The Real Lincoln*, those who opposed Jackson split off from the Democratic-Republican Party to become the Whig-Republicans, while Jackson and his allies remained Democrats. His opponents labeled him a "jackass," and the president liked the name so much that it became the symbol of the Democratic Party.[31]

DiLorenzo tells us that Jackson was against the system of British mercantilism, which he felt was being forced on the US by advocates of a centralized government, under which Congress would subsidize corporations (corporate welfare). Jackson took James Madison's view that "the general welfare clause of the constitution was never intended to become a Pandora's Box for special interest legislation." Thus, we are told

---

[30] Ibid.

[31] DiLorenzo, Thomas. *The Real Lincoln: A New Look at Abraham Lincoln.* Crown Forum, 2003.

that when Jackson became president, he used his veto power to wipe out all internal improvement bills, referring to them as "saddling ... the government with the losses of unsuccessful private speculation." DiLorenzo further informs us that in Jackson's Farewell Address, he bragged that he had "finally overthrown ... this plan of unconstitutional expenditure for corrupt influence."[32]

Andrew Jackson was also against protectionist tariffs, which he felt favored big business, and he offered a bill to abolish the electoral college, as he was in favor of the popular vote. He also wanted to abolish the bureaucracy that remained in power when a new president was elected, allowing them to be replaced with loyal allies of the new president. In his battle against the Second Bank of the United States, which was the legacy of centralized government advocates like Alexander Hamilton and Henry Clay, Jackson tried to push a banking charter through Congress. President Jackson labeled the bank as a corrupt, elitist institution that manipulated paper money and had too much power over the economy. In 1836, he issued the Specie Circular, which required payment in gold and silver for the purchase of public lands.

Jackson won the battle in the end when the bank was boarded up, but after the death of President William Henry Harrison after only a year in office (1841), John Tyler continued the fight with the Whigs over whether a strong central government would be more beneficial than increased states' rights. This argument had caused President Jackson's vice president, John Calhoun, to resign when Jackson sided with South Carolina in the nullification crisis of 1832, in which South Carlina threatened to secede from the Union over high protectionist tariffs.

Jackson's views angered his opponents. A house painter attempted to shoot the president at a ceremony at the Capitol, but when the second gun didn't go off, Old Hickory rushed the man and beat him with his cane.

Andrew Jackson is perhaps remembered best for the controversial Indian Removal Act of 1830, which led to the Trail of Tears. At the time, though, Jackson was a popular leader. However, the reality, according to Alfred Cave in his scholarly article, "Abuse of Power: Andrew Jackson and the Indian Removal Act of 1830," was that Jackson abused his power as president by not enforcing the treaties that already existed and by conniving with Democrat politicians, newspaper editors, state officials, and

---

[32] Ibid.

Indian agents to pass the Indian Removal Act.

In Jackson's mind, the Native Americans either lived in sovereign nations (which they claimed to be) or had to adhere to the state in which they lived. If they were sovereign nations, then they were not adhering to the Constitution and had to break apart.

According to Cave, the Indian Removal Act did not require the Native Americans to move; it gave them the choice of remaining on their lands if they recognized the states in which they lived. Cave claims the Indian Removal Act of 1830 "neither authorized the unilateral abrogation of treaties guaranteeing Native Americans land rights within the states, nor the forced relocation of the eastern Indians." In other words, the president passed the act off as if it required the Native Americans to relocate west, which it did not and was not what Congress intended, which Cave says was an "abuse of Presidential power." Hence, we are told that Jackson "disregarded a key section of the act" and also violated the Trade and Intercourse Act of 1802, which allowed white missionaries, teachers, and tradesmen to operate on Native American land.[33]

Jackson was under pressure from the American Board of Commissioners of Foreign Missions in Boston. This group was a thorn in Jackson's side, and he fought back by using the Trade and Intercourse Act of 1802 to deny missionaries access to Native American land. The act prohibited citizens from entering native territory without a license, and Jackson saw it as a way to prevent humanitarian groups from interfering with his policies regarding the Native American problem.

Cave examined Jackson's December 1830 address to Congress, where he stated that emigration should be voluntary "for it would be unjust to compel the aborigines to abandon the graves of their fathers and seek a home in a distant land." This statement seems to show that Jackson changed his mind regarding Native American removal, claiming that states' rights were superior to federal power. Thus, he used states' rights as a ruse to avoid the issue and did nothing to protect the Cherokee from removal by Georgia officials, nor did he act against the state governments of Alabama and Mississippi when they moved the Choctaw to designated lands in the west.

---

[33] Cave, Alfred A. "Abuse of Power: Andrew Jackson and the Indian Removal Act of 1830." *The Historian*, vol. 65, no. 6, 2003, pp. 1330–53. *JSTOR*, http://www.jstor.org/stable/24452618. Accessed 12 Sep. 2022.

Cave further argues that Jackson hid his push for Native American removal by following his predecessor's policy of granting lands west of the Mississippi to tribes willing to give up their lands. He notes the act provided $500,000 for Jackson to pay for improvements to houses, barns, and orchards but that no part of the act authorized the seizure of Native American lands that they did not cede via treaty.

Secretary of War John Henry Eaton informed Cherokee tribal leaders that their "[claim] of protected rights against encroachment by Georgia was nothing more than temporary grants of privilege awarded by a conquering power—the United States—to a vanquished people."[34] The secretary of war was essentially correct in saying that no treaty could be guaranteed. Ever since the population explosion and the subsequent westward push by settlers, squatters, gold diggers, and land speculators, buttressed by the pressure being put on President Jackson by state officials, made Native American removal almost inevitable. This argument counters Cave's argument that President Jackson abused his power. One can even argue that if he had removed white settlers from Native American lands, he might have caused the Civil War to start earlier than 1860. And furthermore, those in Congress who had the power to create treaties were just as responsible for violating the Indian Removal Act of 1830. Cave tells us the House Committee on Indian Affairs, although it was established by partisan Democrats, "dismissed Indian treaty-making as nothing more than an empty gesture to placate Indian vanity."[35]

According to Cave, Jackson urged his supporters, those in Congress and newspaper editors as well, to portray the act as providing for "voluntary removal" with "remuneration for ceded lands."

Democratic Representative Joseph Hemphill of Pennsylvania proposed an amendment that would have delayed action on the act for a year, pending the report of three impartial commissioners charged with discovering the real wishes of the tribes and certifying the suitability of the western lands designated for their use. But the act passed, with Northern Quakers and Democrats voting against it and most Southern Democrats voting for it.

It is important to put Cave's argument that President Jackson abused his power in the context of the social and political climate of the period. If

---

[34] Ibid.

[35] Ibid.

Jackson had forcibly removed white settlers and squatters from Native American territories to enforce the treaties, this, along with his stand against South Carolina in the nullification act controversy, would have inflamed the states' rights factions that had already threatened to secede from the Union.

In summarizing his thesis on Jackson's usurpation of power, Cave points to the corruption in the removal program, but again, we can say the government was in a conundrum. Jackson could either forcibly relocate the Native Americans to territories west of the Mississippi or allow them to remain in the states, where they would likely be annihilated.

Thus, as we said in our introduction, greed was a major factor when it came to the Native Americans' removal, not only by corrupt officials in the government but also by Indian agents and, to a lesser extent, the chiefs and other Native Americans willing to accept money for themselves and for the resettlement of their tribe. A bit of history tells us that bureaucracies often ignore the wishes of their president and that the president is often between a rock and a hard place, which was certainly the case with President Jackson.

For those who say Jackson hated Native Americans, the context of the time makes it difficult to be certain. Perhaps he did. Or perhaps he was a pragmatist who believed the Native Americans would be better off if they relocated to faraway lands in Arkansas and Oklahoma, where their tribes could live in peace. In any case, the legacy of Jacksonian democracy and Native American hatred lives on.

Andrew Jackson died in 1845 of heart failure and dropsy. His efforts would be carried on by Martin Van Buren, his former secretary of state and vice president, who became president in 1837. According to historian Daniel Feller, we are told that Jackson was grateful to Martin Van Buren for his help in conducting foreign policy with France and Britain and his work in getting rid of the disloyal bureaucracy by replacing them with loyal Democrats.[36]

---

[36] "Andrew Jackson Leaves Office: Martin Van Buren Becomes President." (2014). *Voice of America Multimedia Site.* https://learningenglish.voanews.com/a/andrew-jackson-van-buren/1775693.html.

A political cartoon of President Andrew Jackson carrying Vice President Martin Van Buren into the White House.

President Martin Van Buren continued to support and carry out the Indian Removal Act, praising his predecessor Andrew Jackson for his efforts at moving the Native Americans westward. In 1837, he called the displacement of Native Americans "a settled policy of the country" and said that it was for their well-being. In a message to Congress in 1838, Van Buren stated that "a mixed occupancy of the same territory by the white and red man is incompatible with the safety or happiness of either."[37]

---

[37] Landry, Alysa. "Martin Van Buren: The Force Behind the Trail of Tears." (2018). *ICT. An Independent Nonprofit News Enterprise.* https://indiancountrytoday.com/archive/martin-van-buren-the-force-behind-the-trail-of-tears.

In 1838, President Van Buren sent the army to expel the remaining Cherokee who had asked for more time to prepare. A few hundred Cherokee, without the authority or knowledge of tribal leaders, had signed the Treaty of New Echota in 1835, which stated the Cherokee would give up their lands and move west of the Mississippi within two years. John Ross, the principal chief of the Cherokees, had begged Congress to void the treaty, but his pleas fell on deaf ears. Almost all of the Cherokee were forced to move west.

Chapter 6: Attacking the Muscogee (Creek)

Following the many wars with the Native American tribes in the Southeast and the violation of numerous treaties by the US government, the refusal by the remaining Creeks in Alabama to relocate after their defeat at Horseshoe Bend angered President Andrew Jackson, making him determined to remove the remaining tribes west of the Mississippi. The Creeks had already been pushed out of Florida and Georgia, and now the stage was set for the remaining Creeks (Muscogee) to be removed from Mississippi and Alabama.

But before we get into Jackson's presidency and what they did with the Creek "problem," let's take a look at one of the most prominent Creek leaders. William McIntosh was born to a Scottish father and a Senoia mother and lived on the west bank of the Chattahoochee in Georgia. He taught himself English and blended in well with the settlers and the Creeks.[38]

William was known as Tustunnegge Hutker, or "White Warrior," for his participation in the War of 1812, during which time the Creek Nation split into the Lower Creek and the Upper Creek. McIntosh became the leader of the Lower Creek in southern Georgia, while the Upper Creek resided in Georgia and Alabama. When the Red Sticks split from the

---

[38] Bullman, James A. "William, McIntosh Creek Indian (Muskogean)." https://www.unknownscottishhistory.com/pdf/William_McIntosh_Creek_Indian_(Muskogean).pdf.

Upper Creeks and demanded that the traditional leadership be maintained, the Creeks were effectively at war with each other. However, this war led to the settlers, the US government, and state militias getting involved.

As we said earlier, the settlers encroached on Native American lands, and the government troops and militias came to the aid of the settlers, burning Native American villages and massacring warriors, women, and children. They also enacted treaties that were constantly broken.

The Native Americans did not always take a peaceful diplomatic approach, especially since, to them, it seemed like it would have no effect. They also massacred women, children, and soldiers and burned settlements. These wars were bloody and fraught with tensions.

Chief McIntosh was one of the dissident natives who negotiated treaties with the US government, often doing so without the approval of the Creek National Council. In return, he received large sums of money and land for himself. His actions brought him into conflict with the Upper Creek tribes, who viewed him as a traitor who fraudulently gave away Creek territory that he had no right to give.

The first of the treaties McIntosh was involved in was the 1814 Treaty of Fort Jackson. This treaty was signed after the Red Stick Creek faction was defeated at the Battle of Horseshoe Bend. The terms of the treaty stated the Creek National Council had to cede twenty-three million acres of land in Alabama to the US government. The treaty put an end to the Creek War and saw the dissolution of the Red Sticks, who were forced to move with the rest of the Creeks.

Chief McIntosh fought on the side of the government more than once, including in the fight against the Seminoles. For signing the Treaty of Indian Springs in 1821, McIntosh received 1000 acres in Indian Springs, Georgia, and another 640 acres on the Ocmulgee River. When he signed the Treaty of Indian Springs in 1825, he gave away all the Creek land in Georgia and large parts of Alabama. The payment for this was $400,000, with McIntosh getting $200,000 and another $25,000 for his land at Indian Springs.[39]

For disobeying council law, Chief McIntosh was hunted down by his old enemy, Upper Creek Chief Menawa. In 1825, two hundred warriors

---

[38] Ibid.

set McIntosh's house on fire. He was pulled from the flames and was stabbed and shot to death. Other signees of the treaty were also targeted.

After the murder of Chief McIntosh, the leader of the Creek National Council, Opothle Yoholo, and a delegation of Upper Creeks traveled to Washington to appeal to "the Great White Chief," President John Quincy Adams. Opothle told the president the treaty had been signed without the people's consensus in mind. The president agreed with the Upper Creek delegation, saying the Treaty of Indian Springs should be made invalid.

A new treaty was established, the Treaty of Washington (1826), which gave all land east of the Chattahoochee River to the Creeks for a one-time payment of $217,600 and a yearly annuity of $20,000. It also provided funds for the Creeks to search for new lands west of the Mississippi and to relocate.

The governor of Georgia, George Troup, was angered at this turn of events and began to send surveyors to map out the lands ceded under the Treaty of Indian Springs. He also established a lottery for settlers to win allotments on the land in question. President Adams sent troops to enforce the Treaty of Washington. But when Troup called out the militia, Adams feared a civil war might break out. He backed down and allowed the Georgia legislature to renegotiate the settlement, with Troup seizing all the Creek lands on the borders of Georgia. By 1827, almost all of the Creeks were removed from Georgia, and several years later, many of the remaining Creeks would be removed from Alabama.[40]

The Treaty of Cusseta of 1832 divided Creek lands into allotments so they could either sell their allotments for money to move west or remain and obey state laws. Squatters didn't care what the treaties said and continued moving into Creek lands. By 1836, the Creeks had had enough. They rebelled against the land speculators and squatters and began the Second Creek War.

During this Creek uprising in Alabama, all the tensions between the land speculators, settlers, Native Americans, and the US government boiled over. As more and more Native American land was taken, various tribes began attacking and murdering white settlers. When President Jackson heard the news, he sent Francis Scott Key to assess the situation. Key reported that he found towns growing on Native American lands and

---

[40] "Trail of Tears: Creek Dissolution," (2002).

documented numerous cases of fraud.[41]

The situation was out of control, with both sides committing heinous acts. President Jackson used the violence as justification to move the Creeks west. Some were bound in chains and marched to Montgomery, where they were then put on boats. Those Creeks who were seen as friendly were also forced to move.

---

[41] "The Creek War of 1836 in Alabama, Georgia, and Florida." https://exploresouthernhistory.com/secondcreekwar.html.

Chapter 7: The Original Death March? The Trail of Tears

Historian William Higginbotham, who says he did twenty years of research into government, military, and Cherokee records, claims that Gaston Litton, an archivist at the University of Oklahoma, said a Choctaw heard the phrase "Trail of Tears" used by another Choctaw who was speaking to a Baptist preacher. The phrase was about a road in Indian Territory, and after that, the term spread like wildfire. Higginbotham says the Native Americans in the mid-1800s never used the term and that it is a sleight-of-hand trick by cultural Marxists to slander Andrew Jackson. Such is revisionist historiography, which generally contradicts the gatekeeper's version of historical knowledge, but even if what Higginbotham says is true, the phrase can still apply to the plight of the Five Tribes as they moved west.[42]

It is true that an argument was made by government commissioners, settlers, politicians, and particularly President Andrew Jackson that it would be better to settle the Native Americans on new lands in the west for their safety and to prevent their annihilation by the settlers and the state militias. Higginbotham said it was "to prevent their extinction given that many tribes in the north no longer existed." Another point where

---

[42] Higginbotham, William. "Trail of Tears, Death Toll Myths Dispelled." *The Oklahoman*, 1988. https://www.oklahoman.com/story/news/1988/02/28/trail-of-tears-death-toll-myths-dispelled/62660437007/.

Higginbotham disagrees with the standard version of the Trail of Tears is the number that died. He argues that nowhere in the records is it recorded that four thousand Cherokee died on the way to Oklahoma; according to him, the number is probably somewhere between four hundred and eight hundred. He notes the Cherokee Nation files show that "the number of Indians departing the East ... is recorded at 12,623 the arrivals West at 12,783. Some stragglers joined on the way."

He also quotes T. Hartley Crawford as having said to the secretary of war in 1840 that the number was 447 and also notes that John Ross, the Cherokee chief, never talked about a large number of deaths on the march to Oklahoma, despite his many trips to Washington. We are also told that Ross's brother was the government supplier for the Native Americans en route to Indian Territory in Arkansas and Oklahoma. A doctor from the American Board of Commissioners for Foreign Missions named Elias Butler, a member of a Protestant group at Harvard, was sent to care for the sick. Supposedly, he was the one who spread the rumor of four thousand dead, which was only hearsay.

One other point revisionist historian Higginbotham makes is the notion of the Cherokee being "forced" to march. According to him, the idea of them marching at the end of bayonets through a cold winter to Oklahoma territory is incorrect. He makes the point that the Cherokee left their homelands of Georgia, Tennessee, and the Carolinas on their own after they requested more time from General Winfield Scott to prepare for the journey. Five thousand had voluntarily gone before them.

Higginbotham does not deny the Native Americans suffered but also states that Jackson and Van Buren were sympathetic to the Native Americans, as they supposedly believed that it would be better for the indigenous tribes to move westward.[43]

However, we must keep in mind that the move by the Five Civilized Tribes was at a much later date than, for example, the Delaware, who were forced westward to the Ohio Valley in the late 1700s. The Cherokee were better prepared, having John Ross, an educated chief who spoke English, as their leader. Also, as Higginbotham reminds us, the Cherokee were initially paid $2.9 million for the relocation, which was later increased to $3 million by 1849 due to John Ross's persistence.

---

[43] Ibid.

In the late 1700s, the Delaware were forced out of the northeast toward the Ohio River Valley, partly out of fear of the settlers' wrath and partly because they were getting caught up in the various American wars. They were given no funds to move, there were no doctors to accompany them, and there were no supply depots along the way. Historians tell us the Delaware, who lived in parts of New York and Pennsylvania, were led west by missionaries and guarded by US troops, which means they were effectively forced by violence and fraudulent treaties to leave their ancestral homes. Often, the chiefs signed the treaties with an "X," not understanding the ramifications of the document and hoping that a new homeland for their tribes lay ahead.

Revisionist history aside, the Trail of Tears is generally written as a tragic epoch in the history of America because it was one. Some compare it to the Bataan Death March, where the Japanese army marched American and Filipino prisoners approximately seventy miles to Camp O'Donnell, where thousands of Filipinos and hundreds of American soldiers died. Of course, the Native American displacement was on a grander scale. Many men, women, and children died of disease and starvation, while others froze to death or died of other causes along the long trek over land and water. The Trail of Tears is a network of various routes; altogether, they total up to be over five thousand miles.

In the 1830s, the Five Civilized Tribes—the Cherokee, the Choctaw, the Creek or Muscogee, the Chickasaw, and the Seminole—were targeted to move westward. According to Bruce Johansen in his article "Jacksonian Indian Policy," Jackson fought with and against the Native Americans and always intended to remove them from the Southeast, as proven by his refusal to acknowledge Supreme Court decisions in favor of Native American sovereignty. However, that does not prove he did not sympathize with them or that he did not believe they could rebuild and live a peaceful life in Oklahoma.[44]

Johansen says the Indian Removal Act marked a major shift in US relations with Native Americans, as the policy of "segregating Indians within states changed to moving Indians beyond the frontier—to pushing them from sight," thus setting Native Americans on a path of misery in their march west toward Oklahoma.

---

[44] Johansen, Bruce. "Jacksonian Indian Policy, 1818-1832." https://americanindian2-abc-clio-com.ezproxy.liberty.edu/Search/Display/2219984.

In his article, Johansen tells us the first of the Five Civilized Tribes to be forced to march on the Trail of Tears was the Choctaw in Mississippi, who were moved after they were tricked into signing the Treaty of Doak's Stand. They moved west onto lands that settlers already occupied, which were thirteen million acres in what is present-day Oklahoma.

Consequently, the treaty, which promised 640 acres of land to each household, with 320 acres to each child over ten, and each young child 120 acres, was not honored. And as usual, the government refused to intervene. The remaining six thousand Choctaw chose to remain in Alabama and Mississippi, where they were forced to accept the rule of the state governments in return for allotments of land. Finally, after three treaties had been violated, the Choctaw gave up all their lands east of the Mississippi, for which they received no recompense, and their relocation began in 1831. It took three years to complete, and it is estimated that 2,500 to 3,000 Choctaw died of starvation, disease, and exposure to the elements along the way.

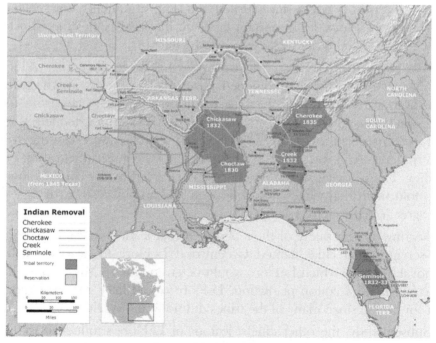

A map of the Trail of Tears.
https://commons.wikimedia.org/wiki/File:Trails_of_Tears_en.png

The Trail of Tears is more than just a trail; it is also a representation of the suffering and deaths the Native Americans experienced as they were displaced. Under pressure from Mississippi settlers who wanted the rich cotton lands the Native Americans occupied, President James Monroe attempted to push the Choctaw out of Mississippi in 1818, with Secretary of War John Calhoun arguing the tribe should decide without coercion. Ultimately, Andrew Jackson was sent to negotiate with the Choctaw, and when the talks failed, he angrily attacked Calhoun and the missionaries whom he said were blocking the removal. With the Choctaw refusing to relocate, claiming that land to the west of the Mississippi was unsuitable for farming, Jackson became more determined to force their removal.

Jackson tried again to force the Choctaw west of the Mississippi. In a second conference held in 1820, a treaty was signed by Chief Pushmataha, with the Choctaw agreeing to give up five million acres in exchange for land in Arkansas. But forcefully pushing the Choctaw west only made matters worse, especially since the settlers in Arkansas were already occupying the designated relocation lands. With the election of Andrew Jackson to the presidency in 1828, the pressure to move the Native Americans out of Mississippi heated up. The arguments now centered around states' rights, an important factor in the legal battles the Choctaw, the Cherokee, and other tribes were waging in court.

The election of Jackson, who expressed his determination to relocate the Native Americans, emboldened government officials in Mississippi, who now felt they had the backing to dislodge the Choctaw from their ancestral lands. In the late 1820s, the state of Mississippi extended its civil and criminal laws over the Choctaw and Chickasaw, outlawing tribal governments. And with Jackson in power, the state government went even further. The Choctaw were threatened and coerced by the commissioners, who told them that whites would pour in and annihilate them if they did not agree to relocate to Arkansas.

Fearing for the safety of their people, tribal leaders in 1830 allowed a self-serving tribal chief named Greenwood LeFlore to negotiate a final removal treaty, in which LeFlore would be given land in Mississippi where he could build a cotton plantation. LeFlore would later go into hiding in fear for his life since many of the tribes did not want to relocate.

Subsequently, the other chiefs, jealous of LeFlore's influence with the commissioners, signed the Treaty of Dancing Rabbit Creek on September 27th, 1830, agreeing to give up the rest of their lands and move to western Arkansas. Under duress and with false promises by the government and the threat of attacks by the settlers, the Choctaw signed the treaty and gave away all their lands east of the Mississippi. As compensation, they were given a twenty-year annuity of twenty thousand dollars with which to build schools, churches, and a tribal council house in Indian Territory.

The harsh terms of the treaty stated that each family would receive one blanket when they reached the end of the trail, that the removal had to be made within three years, and that the families would be given small allotments of land. But the Indian commissioner ignored this last article, denying them the promised land allotments when they arrived. The infuriated tribe threatened an uprising, and LeFlore fled in fear. The US cavalry was again sent in to terrorize the Choctaw into submission.[45]

With the government controlling their annuity funds and government troops watching over them, the Choctaw had no choice in the matter of relocation. In November 1830, the Choctaw, having been led to believe they would be taken care of along the journey, had no idea of the suffering they would endure. For them, the Trail of Tears began in the fall of 1831, and the travel routes varied. Some started at Vicksburg by crossing the river, while others traveled by land to Memphis. Other people took steamboats down the Mississippi River and then up the Red River. Many took steamboats up to the relocation outpost, while others traveled on foot, horseback, or by wagon.

Of course, a frigid winter came, and many Choctaws froze to death along the way. There were no food provisions provided by the government, and if the accompanying commissioner did not buy food along the way, many people would have died of starvation. At the camps near Encore Fabre, Arkansas, there was no shelter and no food supplies, and the temperature was below zero. According to the diaries of the survivors, those who made it to this relocation marker fared a bit better than those who went south toward Louisiana, as many of those who went south got lost in the swamps and had to be rescued by boats. They then went from Monroe, Louisiana, to Arkansas, where they ventured onward to the Choctaw reservation.

Those who traveled to Memphis were afraid to board the boats headed to Arkansas because of a cholera epidemic and decided to travel overland through the Mississippi swamps, intending to cross the White River to Rock Roe, a bayou in Arkansas. While they were crossing the Grand

---

[45] DeRosier, Arthur H. "Andrew Jackson and the Negotiations for the Removal of the Choctaw Indians." *The Historian*, vol. 29, no. 3 (1967). https://www.jstor.org/stable/24442605.

Prairie to Little Rock, a cholera outbreak occurred in 1832, causing widespread deaths.

The surviving Choctaw finally reached the Choctaw Nation in present-day Oklahoma by 1833. The Choctaw experienced great suffering during their forced relocation. They were wracked by dysentery and cholera due to the lack of sanitary drinking water. They had gotten lost in the swamps, supplies were few and far between, thieves stole their horses and livestock, and whiskey purveyors preyed upon the desperate people. By 1836, fifteen thousand Choctaw had been relocated, and the few thousand who remained behind were being harassed. Many of them were forced to leave as well.

The Cherokee who lived in northern Georgia, Tennessee, and Alabama had been forcibly removed from their homelands since the 1820s. Their territory had been reduced by the influx of settlers and the various treaties that had been broken by the state and federal governments. Many voluntarily migrated westward, albeit under pressure.

As was the case with the Choctaw and Mississippi officials, the Georgia government was strengthened in its determination to expel all the Cherokee from the state. In 1828, Georgia took jurisdiction over Cherokee territory, and with the passing of the Indian Removal Act of 1830, it outlawed the Cherokee government, established the Georgia Guard, and took control of gold mines on Native American territory, forbidding them to mine for gold.

With the Cherokee leaders split over the issue of removal and the Cherokee National Council rejecting treaty after treaty, the Treaty of New Echota was signed in 1835 by the faction called the Treaty Party against the wishes of Chief John Ross's National Party. The treaty was negotiated by Indian Commissioner John Freeman Schermerhorn and non-elected officials of the Cherokee tribe. It stated the entire Cherokee Nation would be relocated west of the Mississippi River.

Expecting a harsh winter, the leaders asked for time to prepare. Some, like John Ross, went to Washington to find support and ask for the treaty to be nullified since it did not represent the majority of the tribe's desires. The government did not heed his request, and in the spring of 1838, General Winfield Scott arrived and began rounding up the Cherokee who remained behind. He placed them into camps in preparation for the trek toward modern-day Oklahoma.

The Cherokee faced the same harsh conditions as the Choctaw who marched before them. Water and food supplies were in short supply; measles, cholera, and dysentery outbreaks killed many; and the cold winters took their toll on the hapless Cherokee. Supply depots were set up along the way, and the caravan had a doctor accompanying them, but despite these preparations, the Cherokee suffered just as much as the other tribes in their westward trek.

The waterways in Arkansas were low due to the drought, so the Cherokee were unable to board boats. They were forced to walk, many doing so barefoot, to Dwight Mission, Oklahoma, in May 1834. By 1837, the last of the two antagonistic Cherokee parties, including John Ross and his family, arrived at Fort Coffee, meeting Jackson's deadline of 1838.[46]

However, fourteen thousand Cherokee were still in the Southeast by May 1838. Jackson ordered the state militias to round them up from the disease-ridden camps, where they had suffered in the summer heat. At Ross's Landing in Chattanooga, Tennessee, Lieutenant Edward Deas marched a group 120 miles to Decatur, Alabama, after which they went by rail to Tuscumbia. There, under heavy guard, they were loaded onto a steamboat. Most Cherokees had no possessions since they were forced out of their homes on short notice. After the kindly steamboat operator bought clothes for them, they headed for Fort Coffee in Oklahoma.

The next group of 875 was brought to Ross's Landing, but they were more resistant since they refused to give their names and refused the clothing offered to them. On the route to Lewisburg, Arkansas, hundreds escaped, but 722 arrived by August 1st. With low water levels in the south, steamboats could not be used, and the next party had to travel by road from Ross's Landing to Bellefonte, where hundreds escaped. Finally, they arrived at Waterloo, where a steamboat shipped them to Little Rock. By the time they arrived at the Cherokee Nation in September, 141 had died, and 293 had made their escape. Only three hundred actually made it to Arkansas.[47]

Another group of Cherokees, who also suffered illness and death along the way, were herded overland to Memphis and then once again overland to Little Rock, arriving in Indian Territory in the early months of 1839.

---

[46] Littlefield, Daniel F. "Cherokee Removal." *The American Mosaic: The American Indian Experience.* https://americanindian2-abc-clio-com.ezproxy.liberty.edu/Search/Display/1595705.
[47] Ibid.

These remaining fourteen thousand Cherokee were better prepared for the hazardous journey simply because the removal was more organized by that point. The party had assistant conductors, wagon masters, teamsters, and doctors. Arrangements were also made for supplies to be given at certain points along the way. It is believed four thousand Cherokee perished along the way. The estimates are based on tribal and military records, so unlike what some revisionist historians think, the numbers are not pulled out of thin air.

Chapter 8: Legal Implications and Rebuilding the Cherokee Tribe

The legal implications of the displacement of Native Americans from their ancestral lands revolve around the idea that the Native American tribes had a "natural right" to live on the lands they occupied. There are three various arguments: the issue of Native American sovereignty, states' rights, and the power of the federal government in the making of treaties.

In 1802, the US government guaranteed the Cherokees all the land they occupied within Georgia's territory, provided the Cherokees consented.[48] But we must keep in mind that the encroachment of Native American lands began way before the Compact of 1802. With the arrival of Ponce de León and Hernando de Soto on the shores of Florida, the clash of civilizations began to take its toll on both sides. A tit-for-tat war between the Native Americans and the white settlers lasted for centuries and left the Southeast covered in blood.

Did the Native Americans have a sovereign right to their ancestral lands? It is a legal question that was argued in the US government's executive, legislative, and judicial branches, with tribal chiefs being coerced into signing treaties they did not understand. Many times, the treaties were fraudulent, either through unscrupulous land speculators who sold land

---

[48] Casebeer, Kenneth M. "Subaltern Voices in the Trail of Tears: Cognition and Resistance of the Cherokee Nation to Removal in Building American Empire." *University of Miami School of Law.* https://repository.law.miami.edu/umrsjlr/vol4/iss1/2/.

that was already occupied, government tricksters, dissident Native Americans who claimed to represent the whole tribe, and chiefs who signed treaties in exchange for money and land. At times, the states ignored the rulings of the courts, and the president often refused to enforce the laws enacted by Congress that protected the rights of Native Americans. Therefore, the Compact of 1802 was null and void before it was even signed.

From then on, the Native Americans realized that after years of wheeling and dealing, with lands being ceded to the government and private trading companies, they were ceding too much land and being forced into debt. The Cherokee National Council in 1819 decided to make no further cessions of land. An interesting fact is the different views of land ownership. The Native Americans traditionally believed in communal ownership, with an individual family giving the land back to the tribe, thereby giving the tribe implied ownership over all the land. The whites, on the other hand, used "judicial and common law rules and institutions," which allowed them to manipulate treaties to their benefit.[49]

Often, the Native Americans could not afford lawyers, and with Georgia passing more and more laws, it became harder to fight the states that claimed sovereignty over their land. Georgia practiced a "legal strategy of removal by inconvenience and approved vigilantism; withdrawing criminal law protections ... prohibiting Cherokees from appearing in court ... and making it a crime for any white to enter Cherokee land, by refusing Cherokee gold claims while recognizing white claims within Cherokee territory." [50] Therefore, white missionaries, teachers, craftsmen, and printing presses were no longer allowed on Cherokee lands.

Hundreds of agreements were violated and broken in the 1700s and 1800s. The Cherokees' futile fight for justice continued until 1829 when the Cherokees filed a petition to Congress stating they did not agree to vacate their ancestral lands and demanded the government provide them with legal protection. However, with the election of Andrew Jackson in 1828, they had little hope of succeeding, especially when Jackson pushed through the Indian Removal Act of 1830.

It was around this time that the squabble began between Cherokee officials, with the anti-removal faction, led by John Ridge and Elias

---

[49] Ibid.
[50] Ibid.

Boudinot, now realizing their struggle was hopeless. They began to think the only way to prevent the annihilation of the Cherokee Nation was to agree to resettlement in modern-day Oklahoma.

This brings us to the *Cherokee Nation v. Georgia* case of 1830, with Chief John Ross and Attorney William Wirt (the attorney general under John Adams's administration) arguing that the state of Georgia was making unconstitutional laws that, in effect, would "directly ... annihilate the Cherokees as a political society."[51] Georgia countered by arguing the Cherokee were claiming to be a foreign nation whose rights were being violated. In Georgia's eyes, the Cherokee could not claim the designation of a foreign country since they had no legitimate government. Ultimately, the court ruled the Cherokee Nation was not a foreign country. It was considered a "domestic dependent nation" by the framers of the Constitution and, therefore, had no grounds to bring forward a suit.

Chief Justice John Marshall stated the Cherokee Nation's relationship with the federal government was comparable to "a ward of the state," while Justice William Johnson wrote the "rules of nations" would see the Native Americans as "nothing more than wandering hordes." However, the dissenting justices, Smith Thompson and Joseph Story, wrote the Cherokee Nation had "usages, customs, and self-government" and was a government as designated by the Congressional Act of 1802. This meant the Supreme Court had jurisdiction over the case. The two justices argued the Cherokee suit for injunction against the state of Georgia should be granted.[52]

One year after this case, in 1832, the legal challenge brought by Reverend Worchester against Georgia reached the Supreme Court. In this case, the Cherokee finally received what they perceived as a victory, with the court ruling they were a sovereign nation. Cherokee leader Elias Boudinot, a writer and newspaper editor, rejoiced, proclaiming Georgia's law was declared to be null and void by the highest judicial tribunal in the country. The Cherokees celebrated with rejoicing and dancing. However, the court decision did not prevent Georgia from keeping Reverend Worchester in jail (he refused to take a pardon so he could bring the case to the Supreme Court). Georgia also ignored the Supreme Court's ruling.[53]

[51] "Cherokee Nation v. Georgia." https://en.wikipedia.org/wiki/Cherokee_Nation_v._Georgia.

[52] Ibid.

[53] Casebeer, Kenneth M. "Subaltern Voices in the Trail of Tears: Cognition and Resistance of the

The irony is that the federal government under President Jackson refused to intervene, claiming the state of Georgia was a sovereign entity, as proven by Justice Marshall's previous decision in *McCulloch v. Maryland*, where Marshall recognized the power of a state to preempt or forestall the actions of the federal government. In the case of *Worchester v. Georgia*, Jackson deferred to Marshall's decision, which he claimed limited his power regarding the state of Georgia, thereby giving Georgia tacit permission to continue its displacement of the Cherokees and setting a precedent for future nullification.

Regarding the decision in *Worcester v. Georgia* and Georgia's refusal to obey the Supreme Court, Andrew Jackson reportedly said to General John Coffee that "The decision of the Supreme Court has fallen stillborn, and they find that it cannot coerce Georgia to yield to the mandate."[54]

In summing up the legal battles of the Cherokee against the state of Georgia in 1831 and 1832, we can point to a passage in "Subaltern Voices in the Trail of Tears" ("subaltern" being the voices of the Native Americans crying out for help against an imperialist giant):

> "The States persecuted the Cherokees and asserted territorial control over the Nation, foreclosed a law strategy via state courts, forced the Law strategy into federal courts where the nation was denied sufficient vindication of sovereignty until too late to change the political deluge and denied enforcement of the federal law of treaties by the Constitution ... although the federal courts were open to protect the rights of American [white] citizens derived from Cherokee sovereignty."[55]

But despite everything the Cherokee suffered over a twenty-year period, they were able to rebuild their nation after arriving in Arkansas and Oklahoma. In the winter of 1838, John Ross and his wife, Elizabeth or "Quatie," who was seriously ill at the time, made their way west. She died on the *Victoria*, a steamboat that Ross had purchased for part of the journey, just before reaching Little Rock. She was buried in Little Rock

Cherokee Nation to Removal in Building American Empire." *University of Miami School of Law.* https://repository.law.miami.edu/umrsjlr/vol4/iss1/2/.

[54] Boulware, Tyler. "Cherokee Indians." *New Georgia Encyclopedia*, 20 January 2009, https://www.georgiaencyclopedia.org/articles/history-archaeology/cherokee-indians/.

[55] Casebeer, Kenneth M. "Subaltern Voices in the Trail of Tears: Cognition and Resistance of the Cherokee Nation to Removal in Building American Empire." *University of Miami School of Law.* https://repository.law.miami.edu/umrsjlr/vol4/iss1/2/.

Cemetery. Ross arrived in the early months of 1839, and the unification of the Western and Eastern Cherokee began. By September, they had ratified a constitution, built a courthouse, and established newspapers, schools, and businesses. Once the Civil War broke out, things changed drastically for everyone in the country, and the Cherokee Nation was no exception.

Chapter 9: Historical Legacy

While all the key decisions that led to the Trail of Tears and their outcomes could fill multiple books, there are a few that had a lasting impact on the American landscape, which at the time was rapidly expanding westward.

We can start by looking at the Spanish settlers who settled in the territory of modern-day Florida in the 1500s and how these explorers clashed with the Seminoles who occupied the territory. Ponce de León was killed when he returned to Florida in 1521 to search for the mythical Fountain of Youth, but he was followed by Hernando de Soto, who died of one of the diseases the settlers brought with them.[56]

We are told that smallpox, measles, malaria, and yellow fever killed over 90 percent of the Native Americans in North America, and this was, in a way, one of the causes of the Trail of Tears. Diseases wiped out settlements and entire tribes, leading to groups banding together or fighting against each other for more territory. Siding with the colonists ended up becoming essential in some cases because the Native Americans did not have the numbers to deal a decisive victory on their own. And with their decline in numbers, it became easier and easier for the white settlers to dictate decisions since they were the majority.

Spain finally ceded Florida to the US after signing the Adams-Onís Treaty of 1819. By this point, Andrew Jackson had already made incursions into the territory to stop the Seminoles from raiding settlers

---

[56] "Collision of Worlds." https://www.semtribe.com/stof/history/CollisionofWorlds.

outside of Florida. Jackson was told to invade Florida to go after the Native Americans but to leave Spanish forts alone. The primary reason for the Seminole attacks on the Florida-Georgia border was retaliation for Southern militia coming into their territory to capture escaped slaves. The Seminoles also wanted to prevent settlers from stealing land and cattle.

The Southern states, particularly Georgia, put pressure on the US government, urging it to subdue the Seminole. And this was when Jackson entered the picture. The Treaty of Payne's Landing in 1832 urged the Seminoles to move west if they could find good land, but the scouts could not find livable territory. The treaty was signed, but many chiefs were bullied into doing it, so they continued to resist relocation. After the Adams-Onís Treaty, the US, which had full control of Florida, used the idea of Manifest Destiny to relocate the Seminoles. Ultimately, the decision was made to remove all the Seminoles from Florida, paving yet another path on the Trail of Tears.

In 1820, General Andrew Jackson and Thomas Hinds oversaw the Treaty of Doak's Stand, in which the Choctaw of Mississippi agreed to give up one-third of their land for a million acres in the west. The Choctaw removal began, and the point of no return was reached by the Native American tribes, who were losing the fight against the US government. Before this, one-fourth of the Cherokee Nation had voluntarily agreed to relocate to Arkansas territory, settling between the Arkansas and White Rivers. This intensified their struggle with the Osage, a struggle that had been going on since the 1760s when the Western Cherokee began moving to Osage territory.

In 1817, the Western Cherokee carried out a revenge attack on their traditional enemies, the Osage, massacring the village of Pasuga at Claremore Mound in present-day Rogers County, Oklahoma. The Osage were further incensed when they were forced to cede more territory under the Treaty of Fort Gibson in 1825, and their historical struggle with the Cherokee began once again after the passage of the Indian Removal Act in 1830 when the Eastern Cherokee were forced to move west.

Another key decision that led to the Trail of Tears that is often overlooked was the Louisiana Purchase in 1803. Thomas Jefferson made a deal with France in which the US purchased over 800,000 square miles of land west of the Mississippi for fifteen million dollars. After the purchase, the gradual process of expelling Native Americans from Louisiana began in 1803, lasting until 1840. Jefferson's idea was for the Native Americans in

Louisiana, including the Choctaw and the Natchez, to assimilate into European culture. If they resisted, they should be removed. But this was not to be since most were removed from Louisiana by treaties.

The Supreme Court rulings in the *Cherokee Nation v. Georgia* and *Worchester v. Georgia* led to important decisions involving the issue of federalism. The issue is a complicated one, but essentially, federalism or decentralization is the division of powers between the federal government and the state governments, with the Constitution as the arbiter.

To quickly recap the cases, the Supreme Court dismissed the first case brought by the Cherokee Nation, saying that it lacked merit because the Cherokee did not have the standing to claim sovereignty because it was not a foreign nation. In the second ruling (*Worchester v. Georgia*), the Supreme Court said because the Cherokee Nation had a government, it did have sovereignty. This decision angered the state of Georgia, which ignored the decision and continued to displace the Native Americans, with the president, Andrew Jackson, doing nothing to enforce the Supreme Court ruling.

These decisions caused the issue of slavery to flare up and rallied calls to abolish slavery. Andrew Jackson was a supporter of slavery (he owned slaves himself, as did the Cherokee and other Native Americans) and, thus, opposed the abolitionist movement. President Jackson had widespread support among Northern and Southern Democrats who supported slavery during his time as president, but the calm that ensued after the Missouri Compromise (1820) was now turning into a storm over slavery, mostly caused by Northern agitators spreading propaganda throughout the South.[57]

The fires were again stoked when Mexico freed its slaves in 1829, frightening the slaveholders in Texas, which was still part of Mexico at the time, and by the publication of the *Liberator* by William Lloyd Garrison, a Northern abolitionist, in 1831. In the fall of that year, the Nat Turner rebellion in Virginia occurred. Sixty white citizens were massacred, inciting tensions between slaveholders and defenders of the institution and those who wished to either dismantle it or decrease its influence, especially in newly created states. The discussion over slavery led to arguments about states' rights and the possible dissolution of the Union. Jackson, a

---

[57] Henig, Gerald S. "The Jacksonian Attitude Toward Abolitionism in the 1830s." *Tennessee Historical Quarterly*, vol. 28, no. 1, 1969, pp. 42-56. *JSTOR*, http://www.jstor.org/stable/42623057.

slaveowner and defender of states' rights, was at the time supported by his vice president, Martin Van Buren. Later, to maintain the support of Southerners, Van Buren stated in his 1837 Inaugural Address that "slavery must be left to the control of the slaveholding states themselves, without molestation or interference from any quarter."

Even the famous American writer James Fenimore Cooper, who wrote *The Last of the Mohicans*, supported President Jackson in his belief that states should regulate their own affairs, saying that "Congress did not have the power to interfere with slavery and that it rested entirely with the different states."[58]

So, we can see how the events of the early 1800s, the treaties with Native Americans, the court battles for Native American rights, and the displacement of the tribes to Oklahoma came to play a role in the future of America. States' rights and the power of Congress and the executive branch to control the states on certain issues were discussions that were held during the Native American removal. The people began to see that the states had more rights, and when that idea began to be infringed upon by the US regarding slavery, there were many people who were not happy.

Regarding the rise of the anti-removal movement, we are told by Mary Hershberger in her scholarly article titled "Mobilizing Women, Anticipating Abolition: The Struggle Against Indian Removal in the 1830s" that women across the country signed petitions defending the rights of Native Americans, saying that not only were they protected by previously signed treaties but also that they had become successful farmers and tradesmen. The first two prominent women opposing the Indian Removal Act were Catharine Beecher and her sister Harriet Ward Stowe (the future author of *Uncle Tom's Cabin*), who launched a petition drive in which many Americans protested the Indian Removal Act.[59]

Hershberger states that President Van Buren was stunned by the power of the anti-removal forces. The outcry and surge of petitions exasperated him, but he was determined to carry out Jackson's removal policy because Jackson had previously said that "no other subject was of greater importance than this." Hershberger argues that "the heart of Indian land

---

[58] Ibid.

[59] Hershberger, Mary. "Mobilizing Women, Anticipating Abolition: The Struggle against Indian Removal in the 1830s." *The Journal of American History*, vol. 86, no. 1, 1999, pp. 15–40. *JSTOR*, https://www.jstor.org/stable/2567405. Accessed 7 Oct. 2022.

policy had always been nothing less than land cessions to white markets, and treaties were the preferred weapon," ignoring the possibility of civil war if Jackson or Van Buren had used military force to remove white squatters from Native American lands.[60]

As we noted earlier, Jackson was being hammered by all sides, and Hershberger lays out in her critique the quandary that Jackson was in by stating the two rationales Jackson offered for removal. Firstly, "having an independent Indians nation residing within the borders of any state was an intolerable situation. And second, "that for their survival, southeastern Indians had to move across the Mississippi away from white encroachment."[61] The question of Jackson's sincerity is comparable to asking why Winston Churchill, a staunch anti-communist, suddenly embraced Joseph Stalin in WWII.

As we said earlier, in Jackson's Inaugural Address, he opposed Native American removal but began to embrace the idea in his first year of office. Were these his thoughts from his early days as a fighter against Native Americans? It's impossible to say, but the fact is that he pushed the Indian Removal Act of 1830 over the objections of religious organizations and missionary outposts around the country.

The voluntary women's associations teamed up with religious institutions and their missionaries. A flurry of petitions was sent to Congress. As Hershberger tells us, the anti-removal movement merged with the abolitionist movement, with many activists realizing that removing Native Americans would be akin to removing blacks to Africa. Thus, the colonization movement became the abolitionist movement, and women's auxiliary organizations, together with the missionaries, took up the fight against Jackson's and Van Buren's Indian Removal Act.

Hershberger tells us that women who had no standing adopted a feeling of "Republican motherhood," using petitions in defense of widow's pensions, employment for the needy, and what they considered to be the inhumane act of Native American removal. They became, in effect, "the moral guardians of the nation's virtue," with one of their priorities being the establishment of Native American schools in the Northeast and the South. They did this by funding religious organizations and missionaries who established schools. One of the first missionary commissions was

---

[60] Ibid.

[61] Ibid.

given to Charles Finney by the Utica Female Missionary Society in 1824.[62]

The denominational periodicals countered the arguments of critics who said the Native Americans were facing "extinction" by pointing to the numerous Cherokee schools and teachers, their commerce, and their widespread agriculture. The periodicals further argued the shame of the nation could be seen in the numerous massacres committed by white citizens, with several of them pointing to the 1782 massacre of over ninety Moravians in the village of Gnadenhutten in Ohio by a mob of whites. All the harsh acts carried out against the Native Americans were being published in these nationwide periodicals, and Jackson's election caused a spike in protests and an outpouring of sympathy for the Native Americans in these publications.

In 1829, the American Board of Commissioners for Foreign Missions led by Jeremiah Evarts printed the "William Penn Essays" in the *National Intelligencer,* outlining the treaties between the Native Americans and the US government and claiming that the Native Americans legally owned their land.

These essays were published around the country, even in the *Cherokee Phoenix.* Joyous sentiments were expressed by *The Journal of Commerce* and *the Christian Watchman,* saying the entire nation should "notice the feeling which is now excited in the community about the rights of the Aborigines of this country." Hershberger's research tells us the "William Penn Essays" were more popular than Thomas Paine's *Common Sense* and led to the two famous Supreme Courts cases of Cherokee *Nation v. Georgia* and *Worcester v. Georgia* and the rise of the women's movement that tied the anti-removal movement to the developing abolitionist movement. But despite these efforts, the Indian Removal Act passed, and the Supreme Court ruling in favor of Native American sovereignty was ignored by Georgia, with President Jackson turning a blind eye.[63]

Later, in 1837, the Pinckney Gag rule passed by Congress was designed to table anti-slavery petitions and stated that Congress had no right to interfere with slavery. Hershberger tells us that Catharine Beecher, who did her best to remain anonymous during the campaign, had a breakdown over the stress involved in petitioning and ultimately gave up the fight. She went into mainstream politics.

---

[62] Ibid.

[63] Ibid.

Thus, the events that occurred before and during the Jackson and Van Buren presidencies led to the virtual disappearance of the back to Africa movement (colonialist movement), which evolved into the nullification crisis of 1832 and the abolitionist movement, which as Henig states, "was one of the major ingredients prompting the transition of South Carolina from extreme nationalism in 1816 to extreme sectionalism in 1836."[64] Hence, we can see how the events that occurred in history between 1830 and 1850 led to a bloody civil war over the issues of tariffs placed on cotton (states' rights) and the anti-slavery movement (which stemmed from the anti-removal movement).

And with the Civil War, history witnessed the North's victory, which put an end to the Confederacy and brought about the abolition of enslaved people. No one can argue that the Civil War did not alter the course of American history, as it brought about the Thirteenth, Fourteenth, and Fifteenth amendments to the US Constitution.

So, we can see how events that occurred a few hundred years ago shaped the legal, social, economic, and political landscape of America, which would eventually become an economic powerhouse in the world. As was noted earlier, the Native Americans did not fare too well in their quest for sovereignty, as their legal battles were stymied at every point, while the slaves were only fully freed at the end of the Civil War. Both groups of people still had to fight for their rights after the bloodshed stopped.

---

[64] Henig, Gerald S. "The Jacksonian Attitude Toward Abolitionism in the 1830s." *Tennessee Historical Quarterly*, vol. 28, no. 1, 1969, pp. 42–56. *JSTOR*, http://www.jstor.org/stable/42623057.

Chapter 10: Legendary Figures

Many important figures appeared during our journey through this time in American history, but in the looking glass, a few stand out.

"Mad" Anthony Wayne

When we read about George Washington and his struggle with Native American policies, historians tell us that he often sent General "Mad" Anthony Wayne to quell the disturbances. Mad Anthony, whose prominence stands out for his performance in the Revolutionary War, fought alongside General Washington and Marquis de Lafayette. General Wayne got his nickname when one of his spies was arrested for disorderly conduct in a small town. The general ordered that the lad be given twenty-nine lashes, and thereafter, the men called the general "Mad Anthony."[65]

When summoned by Washington to put down the Northwest Indian War, Wayne took a year to train his troops, which he called the Legion of the United States, and marched up to western Ohio to defeat Blue Jacket, the Shawnee war chief, in the Battle of Fallen Timbers in 1794. He then went on to negotiate the Treaty of Greenville (1795), which ended all tribal claims to Ohio and the surrounding areas.

President Washington believed the Native Americans could be civilized, but that if that turned out not to be possible, bloodshed would be necessary. The next president, John Adams, felt that Native American removal should be voluntary, but over time, he supported thirty treaties

---

[65] Hickman, Kennedy. "American Revolution: Major General Anthony Wayne." ThoughtCo, Aug. 28, 2020, https://thoughtco.com/major-general-anthony-wayne-2360619.

that required Native Americans to give up the titles to their lands.

Thomas Jefferson

If we move on to the thinking of the third president, Thomas Jefferson, we can gain a deeper understanding of what shaped his thinking about the Native American "problem."

In Andrea Petrini's essay, "The Enlightenment of Thomas Jefferson," we are told Jefferson was schooled in the philosophy of the European Enlightenment, which meant he believed "the laws of human society and the physical world [can] be discerned through the scientific method." Quoting the American scholar Joseph Blau, he wrote that Jefferson believed that "open eyes and an active mind—enlightenment—were available to every man and were the guarantees of a good life." Jefferson later applied these thoughts to the American Revolution, believing that Americans should be free from the whims of the king of England and be able to express their natural rights in a "truly democratic society."[66]

Following the American Revolution, Jefferson began to theoretically apply these thoughts to the Native Americans, believing they could become civilized if they only agreed to change their ways, in effect becoming part of European-American society. Unlike Alexander Hamilton, Benjamin Franklin, and others before him, Jefferson never came to believe that blacks could be "equals of whites" but was ambivalent in his thinking regarding Native Americans, whom he believed were higher on the scale of races than African Americans. He even approved the marriages of his daughters to men who claimed to be distant relatives of Pocahontas. While Jefferson never allowed Native Americans to rise to the level of the white man, he began to believe they could be educated, especially when archaeologists in Ohio began uncovering Native American mounds and other designs with squares and circles, as Jefferson had a lifelong fascination with geometry.[67]

Other evidence of his respect for Native Americans can be found in his book, *Notes of the State of Virginia*, where he laments the murder of Mingo Chief Logan's family by white settlers.[68] Jefferson admired Logan's

[66] Petrini, Andrea R. "The Enlightenment of Thomas Jefferson." https://elonuniversity.contentdm.oclc.org/digital/collection/p15446coll2/id/11/.

[67] Kennedy, Roger. "Jefferson and the Indians." *The University of Chicago Press*, Vol. 27, No. 2/3. (1992). https://www.jstor.org/stable/1181368.

[68] Jefferson, Thomas. *Notes on the State of Virginia*. University of North Carolina, 1982 (originally published in 1785). https://www.jstor.org/stable/10.5149/9780807899809_jefferson.

speech to Lord Dunmore in which he said he would never surrender and "cited Logan's eloquence as proof of the verbal sophistication of a people without letters."[69] And while Jefferson spoke of Native Americans in the manner of "remarkable children" and never had a Native American friend, he still, nevertheless, believed they held an "intermediate" level above the race of blacks" though were still "in reason much inferior to whites" and incapable "of tracing and comprehending the investigations of Euclid."[70]

By studying Thomas Jefferson's thoughts on the question of Native American removal, in which he was involved only theoretically, we are given another view of what was going on in the decades before the Indian Removal Act of 1830. Jefferson's "civilization program" was based on making treaties by which he hoped the Native Americans would sell land to make room for white settlers while hoping the treaties would make them loyal to the United States and not to France or Britain.

Jefferson's hope was that the Native Americans would sell their lands, freeing up their hunting grounds on which white settlers could build homes. With their lands gone, it would push them further into debt, forcing them to sell more lands. In a somewhat contradictory letter to William Henry Harrison regarding the Louisiana Purchase, Jefferson encouraged selling goods to natives on a credit plan, hoping to satisfy the white settlers while stimulating the enlightenment of the Native Americans. It is unknown how putting them into debt would be helpful; it seems a dubious form of trickery that was also implicit in many of the treaties.

Still, Jefferson hoped the "enlightened" Native Americans could become peaceful farmers who would assimilate into white society. But again, we are reminded of the overwhelming number of white emigrants from Europe and the frantic push westward that eventually overwhelmed Jefferson's "civilization program" and the supposed "enlightenment" of the Native American tribes. These problems would only grow worse, bewildering and plaguing President William Henry Harrison and those who followed him.

---

[69] Kennedy, Roger. "Jefferson and the Indians."

[70] Ibid.

Elias Boudinot

Elias Boudinot.

Elias Boudinot was a Cherokee born in Oothcaloga, Cherokee Nation, in Calhoun, Georgia, in 1802. His birthname was Gallegina Watie, but he was known as Buck Watie before changing his name. After completing his studies at a local Moravian missionary school, Boudinot was sent to Cornwall, Connecticut, to observe a meeting of the American Board of Commissioners for Foreign Missions, where the goal was to train missionaries to spread Christianity and European culture to young Native American men.

By 1820, he had converted to Christianity after being inspired by his meeting with a New Jersey congressman named Elias Boudinot, who was also the president of the American Bible Society. The young Native American was so impressed by Elias Boudinot that he adopted his name. In 1824, the young Boudinot helped to translate the New Testament into Cherokee by using the system of symbols developed by a knowledgeable man named Sequoyah, a learned Cherokee who studied for twelve years and finally developed the Cherokee language in 1821.

Even though Boudinot lived in a time of racial prejudice, he married a white woman, after which they were burned in effigy. They were forced to return to New Echota.

In 1828, Boudinot published the first Native American newspaper, the *Cherokee Phoenix*, which used the syllabary Cherokee language developed by Sequoyah. He wrote many articles that were against Native American removal. He did write in favor of acculturation, which makes sense given his conversion to Christianity and schooling.

With the Indian Removal Act of 1830, Boudinot changed his views from acculturation and began to write in favor of Native American removal, going as far as to attack Cherokee Chief John Ross, who opposed the relocation of the Cherokees. Boudinot's views brought him into conflict with most of the tribe, as many resisted the idea of moving west of the Mississippi River. Boudinot believed that removal was inevitable. It was clear to him that Jackson would not back down, so it would be better for the Cherokee to secure the best terms for themselves.

In 1835, Boudinot and others signed the Treaty of New Echota, which stated that all Cherokees would relocate to Oklahoma. As we have talked about above, this treaty was not signed with the approval of Chief John Ross. In fact, most Cherokees disagreed with the treaty.

Before Boudinot could move west, he was stabbed to death outside his home. He was not the only one to be targeted. His cousin, John Ridge, and his uncle, Major Ridge, were seen as traitors to the Cherokee Nation. They were all killed on the same day; it is not known who authorized the murders. Boudinot's younger brother, Stand Watie, was also attacked but survived. He believed John Ross was behind it, but Ross claimed to have no part. Stand Watie went on to become a Confederate general. In 1959, Boudinot was inducted into the Georgia Newspaper Hall of Fame.

Chief John Ross

A photograph of Chief John Ross.
https://commons.wikimedia.org/wiki/File:John_Ross_of_the_Cherokee.jpg

John Ross, principal chief of the Cherokee tribe from 1828 to 1866, shepherded the Cherokee, helped them in their legal battles against the authorities, and guided them west to Oklahoma.[71] Born to a Cherokee mother and possibly a Scottish father, Ross learned about Cherokee culture from his grandmother and mother. He later fought with the US Army against the Red Sticks (a faction of the Creeks) after the massacre at Fort Mims, Alabama.

In the following years, Ross helped the Cherokee form a council, traveled to Washington to argue against the persecution and removal of the Cherokee, and helped to build a new Cherokee capital called New Echota in Gordon County in northwest Georgia.

In 1828, Ross was elected the principal chief of the Cherokee. He later assisted Quartermaster Sidney Jesup in negotiating with the Seminoles in Florida and subsequently went on to oppose the Treaty of New Echota in 1835.

After losing the battle to overturn the treaty, the remaining Cherokees began the long journey to Oklahoma in 1838 under the direction of General Winfield Scott. When they arrived in Oklahoma, John Ross assisted in the building of a new capital called Tahlequah, along with many public buildings and schools.

Osceola

Osceola.
https://commons.wikimedia.org/wiki/File:George_Catlin_-_Os-ce-o-
l%C3%A1,_The_Black_Drink,_a_Warrior_of_Great_Distinction_-_1985.66.301_-
Smithsonian_American_Art_Museum.jpg

---

[71] Watts, Jennifer. "John Ross: Principal Chief of the Cherokee People." https://tnmuseum.org/junior-curators/posts/john-ross-principal-chief-of-the-cherokee-people?locale=en_us.

Osceola was a Seminole leader born in Georgia in 1804. He fought in the Second Seminole War in 1835 when General Andrew Jackson was sent in to capture the tribes and forcibly remove them from Florida to the west. He opposed the Treaty of Payne's Landing (1832), as he did not agree with those tribesmen who wanted to emigrate from Florida. In his anger, he murdered Chief Charley Emathla, who had agreed to the treaty, and US Indian Agent Wiley Thompson. Osceola was upset with Thompson's treatment of him. Thompson arrested Osceola for being disagreeable, and to secure his release, Osceola had to sign the Treaty of Payne's Landing.

For the next few years, Osceola and his warriors moved farther and farther into the swamps, eluding US troops and using guerilla tactics and surprise attacks to deal decisive blows on the American soldiers. Finally, in 1837, he and his followers were summoned under a flag of truce to Fort Peyton near St. Augustine to meet General Sidney Jesup. However, it was a trap. Osceola was captured, although most of the others were able to escape into the swamps.

John Horse

John Horse was a Seminole sub-chief. He was an African American Seminole of Spanish descent. To many, John Horse was a brave warrior. He had previously served as an officer in the Mexican army, where he defended free black settlements, and he later fought with Osceola against the US Army in Florida. He fought in the Second Seminole War and worked closely with Coacoochee.

Coacoochee

Coacoochee, also known as Wild Cat, was another important Seminole chief. Besides fighting in the Second Seminole War, he was respected as a high-ranking Seminole and thus held many offices in the Seminole community before and after the war.

After years of hiding in the swamps and carrying out guerilla attacks on American soldiers, he met with William Tecumseh Sherman near Fort Pierce in 1841. By this point, Osceola had died, and Coacoochee's father had also died while traveling westward. Coacoochee agreed to be taken to Fort Gibson in Oklahoma.

However, Coacoochee was not content with life on the reservation. He left in 1849, meeting up with John Horse. The two spent the next few years with a Kickapoo tribe and defended the Mexican border from American and hostile Native Americans. While acting as a supposed peacemaker between various tribes, he traveled between Mexico and Texas while secretly trying to build a Native American confederation. In 1857, he died in a smallpox epidemic in Mexico.

Micanopy

Micanopy was another Seminole chief who fought alongside Osceola, Holata Micco (Billy Bowlegs), and Coacoochee (Wild Cat), known as Gato del Monte by the Mexicans.

Micanopy was born around 1780 near St. Augustine, Florida, and he was known as the "Chief of Chiefs," although he wouldn't become principal chief until he was nearly forty years old.

Like other high-ranking Seminoles, he employed former slaves to tend his lands. It is believed Micanopy had over one hundred fugitive slaves in his employment. And like other Seminoles, Micanopy did not see blacks as being lesser. He even encouraged intermarriage between Seminoles and African Americans.

Micanopy supported Osceola in rebuking the Treaty of Payne's Landing and led warriors who annihilated General Francis Dade and his troops when they pursued him into the swamps. The Dade massacre kicked off the Second Seminole War.

In 1837, Micanopy was believed to be meeting with General Thomas Jesup under a flag of truce, but Jesup betrayed and captured him, along with Osceola. He was imprisoned in Charleston, South Carolina, and died soon after he was deported to Indian Territory. He died at Fort Gibson in 1849.

Seminole Chief John Jumper (Heneha Mekko)

A photograph of John Jumper.
https://commons.wikimedia.org/wiki/File:John_Jumper.jpg

John Jumper was the nephew of Micanopy. He was a Baptist minister and became a Seminole chief in 1849. Since the Seminoles had a matrilineal kinship system, after Micanopy passed, the position of chief went to his sister's children, first James (Jim) Jumper and then John. Before this happened, John Jumper fought in the Second Seminole War, leading two hundred warriors against the over one hundred soldiers led by US Army Major Francis Dade, who was sent into the swamps to capture the Seminoles. Dade's troops fell into the trap set by Jumper. Dade and his men were forty miles short of their intended destination of Fort King. Most of them fell in the battle.

Historian Frank Laumer says the Seminoles "made a terrible mistake by attacking the US Army in broad daylight." He further says that it "was an affront that simply could not be born according to the honor system of the time." This insult to the US Army made them more determined to capture the remaining Seminoles. Laumer believes that if this slaughter had not taken place, the Seminoles might have remained on their lands in Florida, as it was a place that nobody wanted. He writes about Florida, saying it was "a pestilential place, full of alligators and Indians. People termed it the most miserable place they ever saw."[72]

John Jumper was eventually captured. He was sent to Indian Territory but was later returned to Florida to convince the remaining Seminoles to relocate to Oklahoma. However, he was not successful, as the remaining Seminoles moved farther into the Everglades.

In 1861, John Jumper made an alliance between the Seminoles and the Confederate States of America. He was given the rank of major and later lieutenant colonel. After the war, he became a Baptist minister. He died at his home near Wewoka, Oklahoma, in 1896.

Abraham

Abraham was a slave born at the end of the 1700s in either Georgia or Florida, and he worked for a physician named Doctor Sierra in northern Florida. His opportunity for freedom arose when a British officer promised freedom to slaves who volunteered to fight with the British in the War of 1812 against the Americans.

By 1814, Abraham was laboring in a construction fort at Prospect Bluff, a British fort that would soon become a place of refuge for escaped slaves

---

[72] Warren, Michael. "Dade's Massacre Reenacts Start of Second Seminole War." https://floridatraveler.com/dades-massacre-recalls-seminole-history/.

from the Carolinas and Georgia. Having spent his life in the wilds of Florida, Abraham had become acculturated with the Seminole people and found a common cause in their struggle for freedom against the US government.

Abraham quickly became a leader and quickly adapted to the customs and language of the Seminoles. Within a short time, he was considered a warrior, and they called him Suwanee Warrior for his defense of a town with the same name.

Back in 1813, he founded the Black Seminole town of Pilaklikaha, also known as Abraham's Town, where he was accepted as a member of the Seminole Nation. Prior to the First Seminole War (1817–1818), Abraham was living at Fort Prospect, also known as Negro Fort, on the Apalachicola River with three hundred escaped slaves and Red Sticks who had fled south from General Andrew Jackson's advances. When the Seminole settlements along the Apalachicola River were seen as a threat by the Southern planters, Jackson ordered the fort to be destroyed. The survivors, which included Abraham, escaped to the British post at Prospect Bluff.

In 1815, Major Edward Nicholls, the Irish major in charge, left for England, leaving the surviving Red Stick warriors and the escaped slaves with most of the ammunition and artillery. A black man named Garcon (some say he was a chief) commanded the fort with an unnamed Choctaw chief. They invited runaway slaves to settle in the fort, which offered protection. Soon, their settlement stretched fifty miles. General Andrew Jackson was worried the fort would only continue to grow, which would make it nearly impossible to tear down.

In July 1816, Jackson's forces and slave-hunting Creeks sailed to the fort. On July 27th, a gunboat shell landed in the ammunition depot of the fort and caught the magazine on fire, creating an explosion. Over three hundred people died, and almost everyone else inside the fort was injured. It is important to note that not everyone inside the fort was a soldier. Women and children were also killed.

The survivors, which included Abraham escaped. The Creeks captured Garcon and shot him. They scalped the Choctaw chief and stabbed him to death. The surviving slaves who weren't able to escape in the aftermath were returned to their owners.

Later in the Second Seminole War (1835–1842), Abraham served as a scout and an interpreter for Chief Micanopy. Not much is known about

Abraham's death, but we do know that he later lived in Bowlegs Town on the Suwannee River and later married the widow of Billy Bowlegs.

General Thomas Sidney Jesup

The Seminoles were the last Native American tribe to be forcibly removed from their lands in Florida. Despite embarking on many campaigns, Andrew Jackson failed to dislodge the Seminoles. In 1836, he appointed Quartermaster Thomas Sidney Jesup, whom he considered a man of action, to deal with the remaining Creeks in Alabama and Georgia. He was later tasked with removing the remaining Seminoles, including the Black Seminoles, the escaped slaves who had joined the Seminole Nation, from Florida.

Jesup was born in the frontier county of Berkeley, Virginia, in 1788. His father, Major James Edward Jesup, was a decorated officer in the Revolutionary War. He married an Irish woman named Ann O'Neill, the sister of Colonel George Croghan, a man who received honors for his actions in the War of 1812 when he defended Fort Stephenson.

Nineteen-year-old Jesup joined the army in 1808 and was soon awarded the honor of being a second lieutenant, even though he had no experience. Due to his diligence as an officer, he was quickly promoted to first lieutenant. The fact that he grew up in a military family and lived on the frontier surrounded by hostile Native Americans gave him insight into what the army was doing wrong in its struggle with the native tribes.

In 1818, he was appointed brigadier general and quartermaster and began making plans for forts and outposts. He also found ways to better improve the conditions and morale of his troops. During the Second Seminole War, he was given command of US troops in Florida, which aligned with state militias and friendly Creeks. They had orders to move the Seminoles west of the Mississippi River.

Jesup saw the fugitive slaves as the key to capturing Seminole Chief Osceola, the Black Seminole leader John Horse, Micanopy and his black advisor and interpreter Abraham, Alligator, and Coacoochee. Jesup knew the Seminoles had a great love for the blacks who became part of the tribe. Most enslaved people became successful farmers; their only restriction was that they had to pay an annual tribute of part of their harvest to the Seminoles. Jesup felt that by disrupting the Seminole economy, he could force them to surrender. In a letter, he wrote, "This, you may be assured, is a negro problem, not an Indian war; and if it is not speedily put down, the south will feel the effects of it on their slave population before the end of the next season."[73]

General Jesup.
https://commons.wikimedia.org/wiki/File:Thomas_Sidney_Jesup.jpg

In November 1836, President Jackson appointed Thomas Sidney Jesup to command the American forces in Florida. He was the mediator with the War Department during the Second Seminole War. Jesup's orders were to clear the Native Americans from the banks of the Withlacoochee River in Florida and away from Fort King and Volusia near the St. Johns River.

But the elusive Seminoles slipped away into the swamps as the troops approached. The only thing Jesup accomplished in his first attack was capturing a village at the Hatchee-Lustee Creek, which was filled with women and children who had been left behind by the retreating Seminoles.

Jesup's next attempt to capture the Seminole chiefs and their warriors, which numbered about four thousand, was in 1835 after Osceola attacked

[73] "General Jesup." http://johnhorse.com/trail/02/c/01.htm .

Fort King to kill his hated enemy, Indian Agent Wiley Thompson. Around the same time, his advisor, Micanopy, carried out the Dade massacre, in which Major Dade was attacked by around two hundred warriors. It is said Micanopy's first shot killed Dade, and a little over one hundred US soldiers were killed. Three soldiers survived, although one died of his wounds the next day.

In 1837, Jesup committed what was viewed as an act of treachery against the Seminoles. Under a false flag of truce, he summoned several chiefs to St. Augustine and managed to capture Osceola and Micanopy, although Coacoochee (Wild Cat) and other chiefs escaped. Even back then, this act was seen as cowardly and treacherous, lending support to the Seminole cause.

After failing to subdue the Seminoles, Jesup was wounded in battle in 1838 and was forced to retire, leaving General Zachary Taylor to carry on the fight.

Major Francis L. Dade

Major Francis Dade was born in Virginia in either 1792 or 1793. While not much is known about his childhood, we do know that at some point he joined the army and fought in the War of 1812. He was given command of the Fourth Infantry Unit in 1815 at the beginning of the Second Seminole War. He carried out military campaigns in the swamps between Fort Brooke in Tampa and Fort King in Ocala in 1825 and 1826, pursuing the elusive Seminoles, who were determined to resist relocation.

In 1828, Dade was promoted to major after serving as captain for ten years. When the Seminoles again carried out an uprising, he was ordered to leave his base at Key West and march to Fort Brooke, leading over one hundred soldiers on a campaign through the wilderness to capture the Seminoles who were led by Osceola and Micanopy.

Since the Seminoles had destroyed the bridges, Dade and his men were forced to wade through the swamps, where they were bogged down. The Seminoles set up an ambush on higher ground. They hid behind palmettos and other plants and trees and opened fire on the passing troops.

Major Dade was supposedly killed by Micanopy. Out of over one hundred soldiers, only three survived, although one later died of his wounds. The massacre was the brainchild of the Seminole, who had set the trap by destroying outposts, supply lines, and plantations throughout

1835.

Zachary Taylor

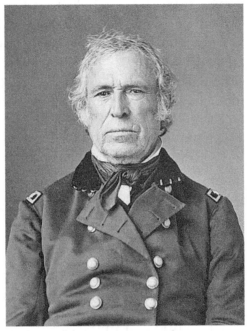

A photograph of Zachary Taylor.
https://commons.wikimedia.org/wiki/File:Zachary_Taylor_restored_and_cropped.jpg

Zachary Taylor, the twelfth president of the United States, was born into a wealthy plantation-owning family in Virginia in 1784 and spent his childhood in Kentucky. He later joined the army and was made a first lieutenant in 1808. He bought a plantation in Louisville, Kentucky, where he owned over two hundred slaves. However, he had little interest in growing cotton and was more interested in guarding the borders against Native American infiltration.

Taylor spent close to forty years in the military, and most of that time was spent fighting Native Americans. He fought in the Mexican-American War to acquire territory for slaveholders and became a hero after his victories at Buena Vista and Monterrey, paving the road for a possible attack on Mexico City. He fought the Shawnee in the War of 1812, fought the resistant Blackhawks in 1832, and in the Second Seminole War in 1837. In the Second Seminole War, he used bloodhounds to track the Seminoles who hid in the swamps. In an 1838 letter, he stated, "I am in favor of [using dogs] ... as the only means of ridding the country of the Indians ... who take shelter in swamps and hommocks ... only to ascertain where they are, not to worry them."

In December 1837, General Taylor, along with eight hundred regular soldiers, two hundred volunteers, and fifty Delaware warriors, fought the Battle of Lake Okeechobee, the largest and bloodiest battle of the Second Seminole War. They went up against approximately four hundred Seminole and Miccosukee on the northern shore of the lake.

General Taylor ignored the advice of his officers and used the same failed tactics that General Robert E. Lee would use at Gettysburg. Taylor employed a classic European frontal assault, hoping to win with a knockout blow. But the warriors hiding in the woods surprised the army as they waded through the muddy swamp. After the battle was all said and done, over twenty-five soldiers had been killed, and over one hundred were wounded. Around twelve Native Americans were found dead, with the rest escaping farther into the wetlands.

Both sides claimed victory, although the Seminoles won the tactical victory. General Zachery Taylor was declared a hero and was promoted to brigadier general. In 1849, Taylor became president.

At the end of the Second Seminole War, an estimated forty million dollars had been spent by the US government, although the actual cost might never be known for certain. An estimated three hundred US soldiers were killed in action. US Army records did take firmer numbers of those who died of disease, noting that 1,145 perished from diseases like smallpox and cholera.

Despite the high costs the US government bore, the Seminoles were never fully forced out of Florida. Sam Jones (Abiaka) declared, "In Florida, I was born. In Florida, I will die. In Florida, my bones will bleach." Although many Seminoles marched westward, there are still Seminoles who live on reservations in Fort Lauderdale, Tampa, and Immokalee.

By the time Tayor was elected president in 1848, the Gold Rush was on, and thousands of would-be miners were cutting a bloody path westward. In a few years, California became flooded with people, and legalized acts of violence were taking place against the Native Americans there.

William Tecumseh Sherman

Another military officer who played a part in the Trail of Tear epoch was William Tecumseh Sherman, the general who used scorched-earth tactics (where everything is destroyed so no one can use the resources there) against the citizens of Georgia in the Civil War. He cut a path of destruction to Savannah and murdered men, women, children, crops, and animals.

Sherman was born in Ohio in 1820. A decade or so before, Shawnee Chief Tecumseh forged an alliance or confederacy of Native Americans in Ohio. Sherman's father was so impressed with the warrior Tecumseh that he named his son after him. His father defended the name given to his son by critics who wanted to know why a boy should be named after a "savage." Sherman's father replied that in his eyes, "Tecumseh was a great warrior."[74]

In all probability, that is likely where his son got his warrior spirit and the idea of using scorched-earth tactics, which Sherman used against the Confederate States of America and the Plains Indians when he tried to drive them out of Mississippi. Sherman put it bluntly to the Plains Indians: "You cannot stop the locomotive any more than you can stop the sun or the moon, and you must submit."[75]

His orders were to make room for the Transcontinental Railroad by moving the Native Americans west, but in the process, he decided to slaughter their food source. Sherman killed five million buffalo to starve the Native Americans into submission, ultimately forcing them onto reservations.

In *The Real Lincoln*, we are told that General Ulysses S. Grant ordered Sherman, the commander of the US Army in 1865, to "conduct a campaign of ethnic genocide against the Plains Indians to make way for the government-subsidized railroads." In 1866, Sherman wrote to Grant, saying, "We are not going to let a few thieving, ragged Indians check and stop the progress of the railroads." In summarizing Sherman's attitude toward Native Americans, DiLorenzo quotes Sherman. When telling his troops what to do when attacking Native American villages, Sherman said they should "not pause to distinguish between male and female, or even discriminate as to age. If resistance is made, death must be meted out."[76]

Sherman and General Philip Sheridan, the Union General who used

---

[74] Andrews, Evans. "9 Things You May Not Know About Willian Tecumseh Sherman." *History* (2019). https://www.history.com/news/9-things-you-may-not-know-about-william-tecumseh-sherman.

[75] Ibid.

[76] DiLorenzo, Thomas. *The Real Lincoln: A New Look at Abraham Lincoln.* Crown Forum, 2003.

scorched-earth tactics in the Shenandoah Valley and said the famous phrase, "The only good Indians I ever saw were dead," committed acts of murder and property destruction under the direction of Abraham Lincoln. Before the Civil War, Sherman fought in the Second Seminole War. Although Sherman expressed remorse for pushing the Seminoles out of Florida, his views were similar to many others in the country. He saw the Native Americans as inferior and standing in the way of progress.

In summing up this chapter, it seems appropriate to quote DiLorenzo about what was happening behind the scenes while violence against Native Americans was being carried out:

"Both the Southern Confederates and the Indians stood in the way of the Whig/Republican dream of a North American economic empire with a subsidized transcontinental railroad, a nationalized banking system, and protectionist tariffs. Consequently, both groups were conquered and subjugated by the most violent means."

He also notes the irony that hundreds of ex-slaves called "Buffalo Soldiers" fought with the army against the Native Americans, "inflicting upon another colored race the ultimate inhumanity: violent death or a concentration camp existence on reservations." Here, we can see the story behind the story that is often not told in history books.[77]

---

[77] Ibid.

Chapter 11: Native American Removal: A Timeline

With all the tumultuous events that took place after the birth of America, the tragedy that befell the Native Americans between the 17th and 19th centuries, culminating with the Trail of Tears, is indeed an important epoch in American history. We asked ourselves at the beginning of our historical journey the question of whether Native American displacement was inevitable, and as we examined the events that took place, one should be able to come to their own conclusions.

The various tribes, particularly the Five Civilized Tribes, were slowly becoming acculturated, in effect adapting to European culture. Most of the tribes switched from hunting to agriculture and became prosperous farmers and traders. Others became Christians, and others became officers in the US Army and were honored for their efforts. Our goal here is not to state whether assimilation was a good or bad thing; rather, we are pointing out that most of the Five Civilized Tribes changed to fit in with American society.

But despite this, the settlers pushed westward, with the US military forging a path of destruction that decimated the Native Americans. Again, we cannot help but note the element of greed within the human soul; the speculators were greedy for lands, the railroad barons were eager for profits, and the gold diggers were hungry for the riches in the soil of Native American territory. Even the US government and the idea of Manifest Destiny can be seen as greedy and hungry for more, more, more, whether that was land, resources, or something else entirely.

So, before we conclude this book, let us refresh our memories with a brief timeline of the major treaties that were signed with Native Americans before and shortly after the Trail of Tears. This list is by no means comprehensive; it is meant to be a short guide to help you retain the information you have read while introducing other treaties that didn't quite fit into the framework of the topic.

One of the reasons we can't delve into all of the treaties is the sheer number of them. From 1778 to 1871, the indigenous people across North America signed around 370 treaties with the US, each of them "based on the fundamental idea that each tribe was an independent nation, with their own right to self-determination and self-rule." [78] But as we have noted several times in the text, westward expansion by white settlers led to violations of most of these treaties. They continued to encroach on Native American lands, fraudulent land speculators granted lands to various tribes that already occupied them, and railroad companies demanded land to transport people and goods west.

Here is a condensed history of the treaties the Native Americans signed:

- Treaty with the Delawares or Treaty of Fort Pitt (1778)

  The first formal peace treaty between the US and Native Americans was the Treaty of Fort Pitt. It was signed by the Lenape (Delaware). It was broken in 1872 when the Pennsylvania militia murdered one hundred Lenape and forced the tribe into Ohio Territory.

- Treaty of Fort Stanwix (1784)

  This treaty gave the US sovereignty over all the Iroquois Confederacy's lands as punishment for their support of the British in the Revolutionary War. The Iroquois Confederacy was divided on signing the treaty and was eventually forced to relocate out of parts of New York and Pennsylvania.

- Treaty of Hopewell (1785–1786)

  Three treaties were signed by General Andrew Pickins and the Cherokee, Choctaw, and Chickasaw, offering friendship and

---

[78] Pruitt, Sarah. "Broken Treaties with Native American Tribes: Timeline." https://www.history.com/news/native-american-broken-treaties.

protection after the War of 1812. They were violated by the encroachment of settlers in the following years.

- Treaty of Canandaigua or the Pickering Treaty (1794)

  The Haudenosaunee (Six Nations), consisting of the Mohawk, Cayuga, Onondaga, Seneca, Oneida, and Tuscarora, signed this treaty with the US government. The treaty gave back a million acres that had been taken in the Treaty of Fort Stanwix, but the treaty was later revoked.

- Treaty of Greenville (1795)

  The Shawnee, Delaware, Miami, and other tribes banded together to fight the settlers. General "Mad" Anthony Wayne was sent to quell the disturbance and defeated the tribes in the Battle of Fallen Timbers. The Native Americans were forced to cede large tracts of what is now Ohio, Michigan, Illinois, and Wisconsin.

- Treaty with the Sioux (1805)

  General Zebulon Pike made an unauthorized treaty with the Dakota leaders, exchanging 100,000 acres for $200,000 to build forts and railroads. Only two of seven tribal leaders signed. Instead of leaving the $200,000 that he had valued the land at, Pike left them with $200 in gifts.

- Treaty of Fort Wayne (1809)

  The Delaware, Miami, Eel River, and Potawatomi tribes ceded 2.5 million acres in Michigan, Ohio, Indiana, and Illinois for two cents an acre. Territorial governor William Henry Harrison later broke the treaty and began attacking the tribes in the Ohio Valley.

- Treaty of Ghent (1814)

  The Treaty of Ghent was between the US and Britain and ended the War of 1812.

- Treaty of Doak's Stand (1820)

  This treaty was said to be a friendship treaty between the Choctaw and the US government. However, Andrew Jackson used threats to get the Choctaw to sign, hinting that the Choctaws would be annihilated if they refused. The Choctaw agreed to give up one-half of their lands in exchange for land in Arkansas and annuity payments.

- Second Treaty of Indian Springs (1825)

  William McIntosh signed this treaty with the US government, agreeing to cede all Creek lands east of the Chattahoochee River. The treaty stipulated that the Creeks would move west of the Mississippi.

- Indian Removal Act (1830)

  Native Americans were promised land west of the Mississippi if they vacated lands in the southern United States. The act broke treaties that were already in place, with the US and state governments resorted to using military force, trickery, or fraud to get the Native Americans to move westward.

- Treaty of Dancing Rabbit Creek (1830)

  The Treaty of Dancing Rabbit Creek was the last major land cession treaty signed by the Choctaw. It was the first Native American removal treaty after the passage of the Indian Removal Act. The Choctaw gave up eleven million acres in Mississippi in exchange for fifteen million acres of land in Oklahoma.

- Treaty of Moultrie Creek (1832)

  This treaty established a reservation for several Seminole tribes in the center of the Florida Peninsula if they agreed to cede all other land claims and capture and return fugitive slaves.

- Treaty of Payne's Landing (1832)

  This treaty was negotiated by James Gadsen and called for the Seminoles in Central Florida to move west of the Mississippi. Although the treaty was signed by several prominent chiefs, most were coerced into signing. The Seminoles continued to resist, leading to the Second Seminole War.

- Treaty of New Echota (1835)

  A small group of Cherokee signed this treaty, agreeing to move west of the Mississippi for five million dollars. Most Cherokees claimed the treaty was a fraud, but Congress ratified it in 1836. The US government used it as grounds to remove the Cherokee. The Cherokee were forced to march thousands of miles to Arkansas and beyond, with around four thousand dying along the way.

- Treaty with the Potawatomi (1836)

  This treaty guaranteed the Potawatomi safety on their reservations in Indiana, but they were soon forced to sell the land for fourteen thousand dollars and pushed westward. Forty of them died along the way.

- Fort Laramie Treaty (1851)

  This treaty defined the territory of the Great Sioux Nation of the Dakota and the Lakota (Teton Sioux), who lived in North Dakota, South Dakota, Montana, Nebraska, and Wyoming. The US government did not claim any part of their land. Instead, they sought protection for settlers traveling the Oregon Trail and permission to build roads and forts.

- Treaty of Traverse des Sioux and Mendota (1851)

  Fearing for their safety due to encroaching settlers, the Dakota and Mendota ceded millions of acres in exchange for reservations and $1,665,000, which equals about seven cents per acre. They didn't receive either; instead, the money was given to traders to pay debts, and the reservation offer was revoked by the US Senate.

- Treaty of Washington (1855)

  The Ojibwe were forced to cede their remaining lands for two reservations on which they were allotted private property. Through this treaty, the US government hoped to destroy the tribal communal laws related to land. The Ojibwe were also forced to become farmers but were still allowed to follow their traditions of hunting, fishing, and gathering.

- Medicine Lodge Treaty (1867)

  Following the Civil War, the leaders of the Plains tribes met with the US government to negotiate a treaty that protected their people from violence from the settlers. There were two reservations, one for the Comanches and Kiowas and another for the Cheyenne and Arapahos, but the tribes never signed the treaty. Congress ratified it and then cut down the size of the reservations, withheld payments, and prevented hunting.

- Treaty of Fort Laramie (1868)

  This treaty established the Great Sioux Reservation (now called Standing Rock Reservation) for the Dakota, Lakota, and Nakota Nations, along with the Arapaho. It protected the Black Hills and comprised all of South Dakota west of the Missouri River. The treaty was violated in 1874 when gold was discovered in the Black Hills, after which white settlers were given miners' rights. Disputes continue to this day over the Dakota Access Pipeline, which is built on the Standing Rock Reservation.

Although there are many other treaties and events that could be included in this timeline, it still gives us a clear view of the United States' drive to expand westward via the idea of Manifest Destiny. By studying this timeline, we can see how the Native Americans stood in the path of what is called progress today. On the other side, we can also see how often the US government violated treaties to better itself and the settlers who were looking for more land.

If we were to elaborate on all of the treaties the US government violated with the indigenous people of North America and the resulting violence that came with that act, we would need at least one more book, if not more. With this brief timeline, we can ponder the facts laid out by John Bowes in his scholarly essay, "American Indian Removal Beyond the Indian Removal Act," which gives us insight into the broader picture of the removal of Native Americans from their ancestral lands. He makes the point that concentrating on the discourse of the 1830 Indian Removal Act, "which is layered in the language of constitutional authority, civilization versus savagery, property rights, states' rights, tribal sovereignty, and government jurisdiction," leads historians to ignore the broader picture of the removal of Native Americans from the East Coast and the Ohio Valley.[79]

For example, he talks about the Delaware, who were forced to cede parts of New York and Pennsylvania, and the Pottawatomi, who were forced out of the Ohio Valley by French, Dutch, and English colonists. On a broader spectrum, Bowes argues that the historiography of Native American removal is centered around "imperium [empire-building] during

---

[79] Bowes, John P. "American Indian Removal beyond the Removal Act." *Native American and Indigenous Studies*, vol. 1, no. 1, 2014, pp. 65-87. *JSTOR*, https://doi.org/10.5749/natiindistudj.1.1.0065.

the Jackson age" and ignores the fact that Americans were "determined to expand geographically and economically" while "imposing an alien will upon subject peoples and demanding their resources." In other words, the tragic story of the Native Americans should not be limited to just the Trail of Tears or those tribes living in the southeastern United States.

Comparable to the plight of the Cherokee, the "Delaware Trail of Tears" was in many ways worse. Not only were they forced to march from their homes, but they also fled in fear of the military violence that was going on around them, such as the Seven Years' War and the War of 1812. The suffering of the Delaware and Cherokee were instigated by white citizens and bolstered by state governments with the implied approval of the federal government.

The Delaware were pushed westward and southward in rapid motion as treaties were violated in accord with the constant influx of settlers. They were forced to march after they marked treaties with an X, which Bowes quotes Richard Lyons as saying that the X was "a sign of consent in a context of coercion."[80]

The Delaware were expelled from the East Coast toward the Ohio Valley. By the 1790s, six hundred Delaware lived between Saint Louis and New Madrid, both of which are in Missouri. They were then forced to escape to Spanish territory in Texas and Mexico. When Mexico declared its independence, the settlers of Texas committed acts of violence against the newly arrived Delaware, who settled along the banks of the Red River in northern Mexico. The Delaware had no permanent home, and the settlers saw them as being in the way.

After the Treaty of Greenville in 1795, the Delaware were forced to move again, traveling four hundred miles by canoe to the White River in the Wabash River drainage, passing their destroyed villages along the way. And yet again, they were pushed out when white settlers flooded the Ohio Valley and the banks of the Mississippi River after the Revolutionary War. By 1822, the remaining 2,500 Delaware living in Southwest missions were given three years to relocate, ultimately ending up with the Cherokee and Shawnee tribes in Arkansas, where they came into conflict with the Osage.

When the flooding in the Ozarks destroyed their cornfields, and the hunting grounds did not provide enough food, the Delaware began to realize they had been lied to. Delaware Chief Kikthawenund (also known

---

[80] Ibid.

as William Anderson) sadly expressed thoughts that could apply to the nightmare experienced by all of the Native Americans: "The white man now claims our country and demands that we should leave it. And now we know not what to do!"[81]

The idea that the US government perpetrated genocide on Native Americans is a controversial argument today. The term genocide is relatively new, having only been in existence since 1944. Yet, just because the term is new doesn't mean that societies in the past didn't willingly seek to exterminate others because of perceived differences. Our goal here is not to take one side or the other; rather, we want you to be able to come to a conclusion yourself while laying out the arguments historians have.

Some scholars say the US government did not seek to exterminate the Native Americans, with many dying of diseases and conflicts that weren't always started with large-scale deaths in mind. Some conflicts started because the Native Americans had committed a massacre or were planning to engage in war.

However, other historians do believe that what happened was tantamount to genocide, and Bowes is one of them. Some of these historians argue that genocide happens when colonization and expansion take place since one group is almost always pushed to the side. It would have been somewhat easy for US politicians to ignore the plight of the Native Americans as long as they pleased the citizens of the country who voted them into power (the Native Americans would not become citizens of the US until 1924). The forced march of the Five Civilized Tribes saw thousands of deaths, many of which likely could have been prevented, although, with such a long journey and the number of people traveling, deaths would have been inevitable.

And even if one concedes that the settlers did not willingly look to exterminate Native Americans, historians point to the cultural genocide that took place. The Five Civilized Tribes is an excellent example of this, as they abandoned many of their traditional ways to assimilate with Anglo-American culture. The missionary schools that popped up across the country also sought to instill Christianity and the English language in children, forcing them to abandon their traditional language, clothing, and much else.

---

[81] Ibid.

Regardless of what one thinks of the genocide argument, almost everyone can agree that the Trail of Tears was a tragic epoch in US history.

Conclusion

Chief Joseph, who became chief of the Wallowa band of Nez Perce in the 1870s, offers a quote that speaks volumes. "I believe much trouble and blood would be saved if we opened our hearts more."

Once most of the treaties with the indigenous people had been broken and their court battles defeated or ignored, there was no stopping the push west by the forces of economic growth. Advocates of Manifest Destiny were determined to crush anything or anyone in the way of progress. This clash of civilizations involved endless arguments over sovereignty and states' rights.

Looking at the plight of the beleaguered Native Americans, we can see that the idea of Manifest Destiny was an uncontrollable force leading to either the removal of the Native Americans to government-controlled reservations or their extinction. Yet, we can't help but ask again, was the Trail of Tears inevitable? Could the deaths and suffering of so many Native Americans be avoided? These are questions that are difficult to ask, and you might not have answers for them right now. But we encourage you to read more about this time in history to come to your own conclusions.

Afterword

We don't hear much today about Native Americans today unless it is a story about a protest erupting over a pipeline being built on a reservation, a fight over hunting rights, or hearing the controversy over a sports team using Native Americans as a mascot or a movie where they are portrayed as savages. Native Americans have the highest poverty rate among minorities, despite the casinos they are permitted to build.

The challenges facing Native Americans today include crime, education, voting rights, mental and physical health, environmental problems related to climate change, and the possible extinction of their languages.

Over five hundred tribes that are presently regulated by the government suffer "spiritual and physical violence, societal discrimination, and ... are degraded when they are stereotyped in the media."[82] Since the Great Depression, the Native Americans have not been able to share in the economic prosperity experienced by most of the American population. Around 33 percent of Native Americans live in poverty. Since the 2010 census, the poverty level among the tribes has increased to 49 percent, and as a result, 700,000 or one-third of Native Americans on reservations live in poverty.[83]

---

[82] "Native American Issues Today: Current Problems & Struggles 2022."
http://www.powwows.com/issues-and-problems-facing-native-americans-today.

[83] Ibid.

Some of the issues they currently face are listed below:

- Lack of emergency care and hospitals;
- Multigenerational housing, which can more rapidly spread diseases to other members of the family;
- Job losses due to the recent pandemic;
- Many tribal elders dying off in 2020, leading to the loss of knowledge, language, and connections to history;
- Violence against women and children; 40 percent of women report rape, stalking, or domestic violence;
- Many reservations have a murder rate ten times the national average;
- A 1990 Justice Department report showed 80 percent of physical abuse and rape of Native American women being carried out by non-native people;
- Numerous reported cases of missing and murdered indigenous women.

In regard to the climate crisis, many reservations have valuable resources that are being exploited, including gas, oil, and timber, with some reservations containing gold deposits. Native Americans have stated this exploitation is causing environmental damage to their lands. As a result, many Native Americans are joining social justice and environmental groups to protest fossil fuels, mining, and the installation of pipelines near reservations.

Other notable problems are high school dropout rates, low college attendance, and high rates of obesity, HIV/AIDS, and diabetes. The Indian Health Service (IHS) is underfunded, and the suicide rate for Native Americans between the ages of ten and thirty-four was extremely high in 2019.

Native Americans face issues voting, as there is a lack of polling places. The need to travel long distances to cast a vote is hampered by the lack of transportation. Reservations do not use traditional street addresses, which means their IDs are not always recognized by outside authorities, but with the passing of the Native American Voting Rights Act in 2021, some of these issues have been addressed.

There are only 150 to 170 surviving Native American languages, but they are in danger of disappearing. It has been predicted that by 2050, there will only be twenty Native American languages left. It was hoped that the International Decade of the World's Indigenous People proclaimed by the United Nations would bring attention to these problems.

In "Native American Life Today," Dr. Maria Yellow Horse Braveheart, a Hunkpapa, Oglala Lakota, professor at the University of Mexico, has developed a theory of "historical unresolved grief," or "a psychological wounding ... following the loss of lives, land, and vital aspects of culture." She talks about five hundred years of trauma due to persecution, relocation, and "variations of physical, mental, emotional, and spiritual violence by European emigrants who chose to expand across the continent, in effect decimating the lives of Native American men, women, and children."[84]

According to Yellow Horse, the scars run much deeper, especially since the discrimination continues today. This "collective group trauma," as she calls it, is "passed down on the cellular level," leading to a greater chance of children experiencing increased levels of stress and the potential to develop mental and physical diseases.

One other aspect we will touch on is the struggle for Native American property rights, a battle that is continuing today. There are 6.7 million Native Americans living in the US, with only 22 percent living on reservations under a "federal trust." The rest live in different parts of the country. A federal trust means the federal government assumes all responsibility for the management of the lands. The government essentially acts as the legal owner or trustee through the treaties made between the tribes and the federal government. Federal trusts interfere with property rights and economic opportunities, which negatively impact life on the reservations.[85]

There is a salient quote from *The Atlantic*, an American magazine. Naomi Schafer Riley writes, "Indians have long suffered from what the Nobel Prize-winning economist Hernando de Soto has called 'dead capital.' They may possess a certain amount of land on paper, but they can't put it to use by selling it, buying more to take advantage of scale, or borrowing against it."[86]

---

[84] "Native American Life Today: Understanding the Destruction." https://pages.nativehope.com/native-americans-today#chp1.

[85] Ibid.

[86] Ibid.

Thus, from a historical perspective, we can see that while much has changed for the Native Americans, there is still a lot of progress to be made. They do not have access to the wealth contained in their ancestral lands, and the lack of progress and economic activity has led to continued problems on the reservations where many of them live. By being aware of current events and reading more about historical subjects like the Trail of Tears, people can realize what needs to be done to make sure that everyone lives up to their full potential.

Here's another book by Enthralling History that you might like

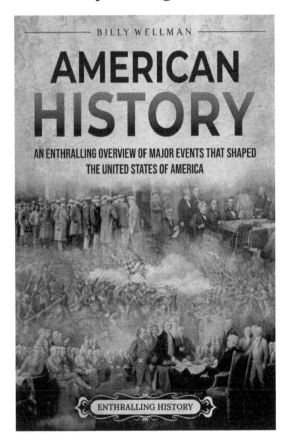

Free limited time bonus

Stop for a moment. We have a free bonus set up for you. The problem is this: we forget 90% of everything that we read after 7 days. Crazy fact, right? Here's the solution: we've created a printable, 1-page pdf summary for this book that you're reading now. All you have to do to get your free pdf summary is to go to the following website:

https://livetolearn.lpages.co/enthrallinghistory/

Once you do, it will be intuitive. Enjoy, and thank you!

Bibliography

Barnett, Jim. "The Natchez Indians - 2007-10." Mississippi History Now, https://www.mshistorynow.mdah.ms.gov/issue/the-natchez-indians. Accessed 9 December 2022.

Champagne, Duane. The Native North American Almanac: A Reference Work on Native North Americans in the United States and Canada. Edited by Duane Champagne, Gale Research, 2001.

"Comanche | History & Facts." Britannica, 31 October 2022, https://www.britannica.com/topic/Comanche-people. Accessed 28 December 2022.

"Comanche (tribe) | The Encyclopedia of Oklahoma History and Culture." Oklahoma Historical Society, https://www.okhistory.org/publications/enc/entry?entry=CO033. Accessed 28 December 2022.

"The Creek War of 1813-1814." American Battlefield Trust, https://www.battlefields.org/learn/articles/creek-war-1813-1814. Accessed 7 January 2023.

"Early Choctaw History - Natchez Trace Parkway (U.S." National Park Service, 4 November 2022, https://www.nps.gov/natr/learn/historyculture/choctaw.htm. Accessed 9 December 2022.

"Encyclopedia of the Great Plains | WOUNDED KNEE MASSACRE." Plains Humanities Alliance, http://plainshumanities.unl.edu/encyclopedia/doc/egp.war.056. Accessed 13 January 2023.

Estes, Roberta. "James Logan Colbert of the Chickasaws and Allied Trader Families." Native Heritage Project, 27 December 2014, https://nativeheritageproject.com/2014/12/27/james-logan-colbert-of-the-chickasaws-and-allied-trader-families/. Accessed 12 December 2022.

Ethridge, Robbie. From Chicaza to Chickasaw: The European Invasion and the Transformation of the Mississippian World, 1540-1715. University of North Carolina Press, 2010.

Grinde, Donald, and Quintard Taylor. "Red vs Black: Conflict and Accommodation in the Post Civil War Indian Territory." American Indian Quarterly, vol. 8, no. 3, 1984, pp. 211-19. JSTOR, jstor.org.

"Hernando de Soto - Facts, Route & Death - Biography." Biography (Bio.), 1 April 2014, https://www.biography.com/explorer/hernando-de-soto. Accessed 3 December 2022.

"History." Navajo Nation, https://www.navajo-nsn.gov/History. Accessed 27 December 2022.

"History & Culture - Sand Creek Massacre National Historic Site (U.S." National Park Service, 29 August 2022, https://www.nps.gov/sand/learn/historyculture/index.htm. Accessed 9 January 2023.

"History: The Navajo." Utah American Indian Digital Archive, https://utahindians.org/archives/navajo/history.html. Accessed 27 December 2022.

Knetsch, Joe. Florida's Seminole Wars, 1817-1858. Arcadia Publishing Company, 2003.

Landry, Alysa. "Martin Van Buren: The Force Behind the Trail of Tears." Indian Country Today, 23 February 2016, https://indiancountrytoday.com/archive/martin-van-buren-the-force-behind-the-trail-of-tears. Accessed 2 January 2023.

Lewis, James E. "The Black Hawk War: Introduction." Northern Illinois University Digital Library, https://digital.lib.niu.edu/illinois/lincoln/topics/blackhawk/intro. Accessed 8 January 2023.

"The Life of Silas Soule - Sand Creek Massacre National Historic Site (U.S." National Park Service, 14 November 2019, https://www.nps.gov/sand/learn/historyculture/the-life-of-silas-soule.htm. Accessed 9 January 2023.

Mann, Charles C. 1491. Knopf Doubleday Publishing Group, 2005.

Martin, McKenzie. "Transylvania Company." ExploreKYHistory, https://explorekyhistory.ky.gov/items/show/384. Accessed 8 December 2022.

"Milestones: 1830–1860." Milestones: 1830–1860 - Office of the Historian, https://history.state.gov/milestones/1830-1860/indian-treaties. Accessed 3 January

2023.

"Mississippi Band of Choctaw Indians." Mississippi Band of Choctaw Indians, https://www.choctaw.org/aboutMBCI/history/index.html. Accessed 9 December 2022.

"Our Culture - Official Website of the Mescalero Apache Tribe." Mescalero Apache Tribe, https://mescaleroapachetribe.com/our-culture/. Accessed 28 December 2022.

"Pawnee (tribe) | The Encyclopedia of Oklahoma History and Culture." Oklahoma Historical Society, https://www.okhistory.org/publications/enc/entry.php?entry=PA022. Accessed 23 December 2022.

"Portrait of Arthur St. Clair." American Battlefield Trust, https://www.battlefields.org/learn/biographies/arthur-st-clair. Accessed 6 January 2023.

"Prehistoric Texas." Texas Beyond History, https://www.texasbeyondhistory.net/plateaus/peoples/apache.html. Accessed 28 December 2022.

"Pushmataha (U.S." National Park Service, 14 September 2017, https://www.nps.gov/people/pushmataha.htm. Accessed 9 December 2022.

"Research Guides: Indian Removal Act: Primary Documents in American History: Digital Collections." Library of Congress Research Guides, 30 September 2022, https://guides.loc.gov/indian-removal-act/digital-collections. Accessed 3 January 2023.

Rozema, Vicki, editor. Cherokee Voices: Early Accounts of Cherokee Life in the East. J.F. Blair, 2002.

Rozema, Vicki, editor. Voices from the Trail of Tears. J.F. Blair, 2003.

Rust, Randal, and Michael Toomey. "Transylvania Purchase." Tennessee Encyclopedia, https://tennesseeencyclopedia.net/entries/transylvania-purchase/. Accessed 8 December 2022.

Seelinger, Matthew. "The Battle of Fallen Timbers, 20 August 1794 – The Campaign for the National Museum of the United States Army." Army Historical Foundation, https://armyhistory.org/the-battle-of-fallen-timbers-20-august-1794/. Accessed 6 January 2023.

"The Seminole Wars." Florida Department of State, https://dos.myflorida.com/florida-facts/florida-history/seminole-history/the-seminole-wars/. Accessed 8 January 2023.

"Settlement, Trade, and Conflicts in Colonial South Carolina · The James Poyas Daybook: An Account of a Charles Town Merchant, 1760-1765 · Lowcountry Digital History Initiative." Lowcountry Digital History Initiative, https://ldhi.library.cofc.edu/exhibits/show/james_poyas_daybook_eighteenth/historical-context-settlement-. Accessed 7 December 2022.

"Shawnee Tribe." Dartmouth College Library Digital Collections, https://collections.dartmouth.edu/occom/html/ctx/orgography/org0089.ocp.html. Accessed 22 December 2022.

"Sioux - The Battle of the Little Bighorn and the cessation of war." Britannica, https://www.britannica.com/topic/Sioux/The-Battle-of-the-Little-Bighorn-and-the-cessation-of-war. Accessed 24 December 2022.

"Stickball." Choctaw Nation, https://www.choctawnation.com/about/culture/traditions/stickball/. Accessed 9 December 2022.

"Story of the Battle - Little Bighorn Battlefield National Monument (U.S." National Park Service, https://www.nps.gov/libi/learn/historyculture/battle-story.htm. Accessed 12 January 2023.

"Tecumseh." Ohio History Central, https://ohiohistorycentral.org/w/Tecumseh. Accessed 12 December 2022.

"Tenskwatawa." Ohio History Central, https://ohiohistorycentral.org/w/Tenskwatawa. Accessed 7 January 2023.

"Tippecanoe Battle Facts and Summary." American Battlefield Trust, https://www.battlefields.org/learn/war-1812/battles/tippecanoe. Accessed 7 January 2023.

"Treaty of Fort Harmar (1789)." Ohio History Central, https://ohiohistorycentral.org/w/Treaty_of_Fort_Harmar_(1789). Accessed 6 January 2023.

"The Treaty of New Echota and the Trail of Tears." NC DNCR, 29 December 2016, https://www.ncdcr.gov/blog/2015/12/29/the-treaty-of-new-echota-and-the-trail-of-tears. Accessed 10 December 2022.

Warren, Stephen. The Worlds the Shawnees Made: Migration and Violence in Early America. University of North Carolina Press, 2016.

Watts, Jennifer. "John Ross: Principal Chief of the Cherokee People." Tennessee State Museum, 2 November 2021, https://tnmuseum.org/junior-curators/posts/john-ross-principal-chief-of-the-cherokee-people?locale=en_us. Accessed 4 January 2023.

Wilentz, Sean. Andrew Jackson: The American Presidents Series: The 7th President, 1829-1837. Edited by Arthur M. Schlesinger, Henry Holt and Company, 2005.

Wilson, James. The Earth Shall Weep: A History of Native America. Atlantic Monthly Press, 1999.

Yarbrough, Fay A. Choctaw Confederates: The American Civil War in Indian

Country. University of North Carolina Press, 2021.

"Abiaka (Seminole Indian Sam Jones) - One of the Greatest Medicine Men in History." https://worldprophesy.blogspot.com/2015/01/abiaka-one-of-greatest-medicine-men-seminole.html.

African American Registry (AAREG), "Billy Bowlegs, Seminole Chief." https://osceolahistory.org/billy-bowlegs-iii-ahead-of-his-time/.

"Andrew Jackson Leaves Office: Martin Van Buren Becomes President." (2014). *Voice of America Multimedia Site.* https://learningenglish.voanews.com/a/andrew-jackson-van-buren/1775693.html.

Andrews, Evans. "9 Things You May Not Know About Willian Tecumseh Sherman." *History* (2019). https://www.history.com/news/9-things-you-may-not-know-about-william-tecumseh-sherman.

Britannica, The Editors of Encyclopedia. "John Ross." *Encyclopedia Britannica*, 28 Jul. 2022, https://www.britannica.com/biography/John-Ross-chief-of-Cherokee-Nation. Accessed 8 September 2022.

Biography.com Editors. "Andrew Jackson Biography." *A&E Networks.* (2017). https://www.biography.com/us-president/andrew-jackson .

Boulware, Tyler. "Cherokee Indians." *New Georgia Encyclopedia*, 20 January 2009, https://www.georgiaencyclopedia.org/articles/history-archaeology/cherokee-indians/ .

Bowes, John P. "American Indian Removal beyond the Removal Act." *Native American and Indigenous Studies*, vol. 1, no. 1, 2014, pp. 65–87. *JSTOR*, https://doi.org/10.5749/natiindistudj.1.1.0065 .

Braund, Kathryn. "Menawa." http://encyclopediaofalabama.org/article/h-3594.

"Broken US-Indigenous Treaties: A Timeline." https://stacker.com/stories/23887/broken-us-indigenous-treaties-timeline.

Bullman, James A. "William, McIntosh Creek Indian (Muskogean)." https://www.unknownscottishhistory.com/pdf/William_McIntosh_Creek_Indian_(Muskogean).pdf.

Calloway, Colin. "George Washington Lived in an Indian World, but His Biographies Have Erased Native People." https://longreads.com/2018/11/07/george-washington-lived-in-an-indian-world-but-his-biographies-have-erased-native-people.

Carlson, Leonard A., and Mark A. Roberts. "Indian Lands, Squatterism, and Slavery: Economic Interests and the Passage of the Indian Removal Act of 1830." *Explorations in Economic History* 43.3 (2006): 486-504. Web. www.sciencedirect.com.ezproxy.liberty.edu.

Casebeer, Kenneth M. "Subaltern Voices in the Trail of Tears: Cognition and Resistance of the Cherokee Nation to Removal in Building American Empire."

University of Miami School of Law.
https://repository.law.miami.edu/umrsjlr/vol4/iss1/2/.

Cave, Alfred A. "Abuse of Power: Andrew Jackson and the Indian Removal Act of 1830." *The Historian*, vol. 65, no. 6, 2003, pp. 1330–53. *JSTOR*, http://www.jstor.org/stable/24452618.

"Cherokee Nation v. Georgia." https://en.wikipedia.org/wiki/Cherokee_Nation_v._Georgia.

"Chickasaw Tribe: Facts, Clothes, Food and History." https://www.warpaths2peacepipes.com/indian-tribes/chickaswa-tribe.htm.

"Chief Dragging Canoe." Video. https://www.youtube.com/watch?v=vrSXzeIXU5M.

"Collision of Worlds." https://www.semtribe.com/stof/history/CollisionofWorlds.

Davis, Ethan. "An Administrative Trail of Tears: Indian Removal." *The American Journal of Legal History*, vol. 50, no. 1, 2008, pp. 49–100. *JSTOR*, http://www.jstor.org/stable/25664483.

"Davy Crockett on the Removal of the Cherokees, 1834." https://www.gilderlehrman.org/history-resources/spotlight-primary-source/davy-crockett-removal-cherokees-1834.

DeRosier, Arthur H. "Andrew Jackson and the Negotiations for the Removal of the Choctaw Indians." *The Historian*, vol. 29, no. 3 (1967). https://www.jstor.org/stable/24442605.

DiLorenzo, Thomas. *The Real Lincoln: A New Look at Abraham Lincoln.* Crown Forum, 2003.

"Early Choctaw History." https://www.nps.gov/natr/learn/historyculture/choctaw.htm.

Feller, Daniel. *The Public Lands in Jacksonian Politics.* Madison: University of Wisconsin Press.

Freeling, William. "John Tyler: The American Franchise." https://millercenter.org/president/tyler/the-american-franchise.

"General Jesup." http://johnhorse.com/trail/02/c/01.htm.

Genovese, Michael A. & Landry, Alysa. *US Presidents and the Destruction of the Native American Nations (The Evolving American Presidency).* Palgrave Macmillian, 2021.

Getchell, Michelle. "Indian Removal." Khan Academy. https://www.khanacademy.org/humanities/us-history/the-early-republic/age-of-jackson/a/indian-removal.

Grose, B. Donald. "Edwin Forrest, 'Metamora,' and the Indian Removal Act of 1830." *Theatre Journal*, vol. 37, no. 2, 1985, pp. 181–91. *JSTOR*, https://doi.org/10.2307/3207064.

Haveman, Christopher. "Creek Indian Removal." http://encyclopediaofalabama.org/article/h-2013.

Henig, Gerald S. "The Jacksonian Attitude Toward Abolitionism in the 1830s." *Tennessee Historical Quarterly*, vol. 28, no. 1, 1969, pp. 42–56. *JSTOR*, http://www.jstor.org/stable/42623057.

Hershberger, Mary. "Mobilizing Women, Anticipating Abolition: The Struggle against Indian Removal in the 1830s." *The Journal of American History*, vol. 86, no. 1, 1999, pp. 15–40. *JSTOR*, https://www.jstor.org/stable/2567405. Accessed 7 Oct. 2022.

Hickman, Kennedy. "American Revolution: Major General Anthony Wayne." ThoughtCo, Aug. 28, 2020, https://thoughtco.com/major-general-anthony-wayne-2360619.

Higginbotham, William. "Trail of Tears, Death Toll Myths Dispelled." *The Oklahoman*, 1988. https://www.oklahoman.com/story/news/1988/02/28/trail-of-tears-death-toll-myths-dispelled/62660437007/.

"History: Chickasaw Nation." https://www.chickasaw.net/our-nation/history.aspx.

Hryniewicki, Richard J. "The Creek Treaty of Washington, 1826." *The Georgia Historical Quarterly*, vol. 48, no. 4, 1964, pp. 425–41. *JSTOR*, http://www.jstor.org/stable/40578419.

Accessed 14 Oct. 2022.

"Introduction." https://www.semtribe.com/stof/history/introduction.

Jefferson, Thomas. *Notes on the State of Virginia*. University of North Carolina, 1982 (originally published in 1785). https://www.jstor.org/stable/10.5149/9780807899809_jefferson.

Johansen, Bruce. "Jacksonian Indian Policy, 1818–1832." https://americanindian2-abc-clio-com.ezproxy.liberty.edu/Search/Display/2219984.

"John Ross: Principal Chief of the Cherokee People." https://tnmuseum.org/junior-curators/posts/john-ross-principal-chief-of-the-cherokee-people.

"Jumper, John (ca. 1820–1896)." The Encyclopedia of Oklahoma History and Culture. https://www.okhistory.org/publications/enc/entry?entry=JU002.

Keating, Jessica. "The Assimilation, Removal, and Elimination of American Indians." *The McGraph Institute for Church Life*, (2020). https://mcgrath.nd.edu/assets/390540/expert_guide_on_the_assimilation_removal_and_elimination_of_native_americans.pdf

Kennedy, Roger. "Jefferson and the Indians." *The University of Chicago Press*, Vol. 27, No. 2/3. (1992). https://www.jstor.org/stable/1181368.

Kievit, Joyce Ann. "Treaty of Dancing Rabbit Creek." *The American Mosaic: The American Indian Experience*. https://americanindian2-abc-clio-com.ezproxy.liberty.edu/Search/Display/1670319.

Knox, Henry. "To George Washington from Henry Knox."
https://founders.archives.gov/documents/Washington/05-04-02-0353.

Landry, Alysa. "Martin Van Buren: The Force Behind the Trail of Tears."
(2018). *ICT. An Independent Nonprofit News Enterprise.*
https://indiancountrytoday.com/archive/martin-van-buren-the-force-behind-the-
trail-of-tears.

Little, Becky. "How Boarding Schools Tried to 'Kill the Indian' Through
Assimilation." *History* (2018): Web. https://www.history.com/news/how-boarding-
schools-tried-to-kill-the-indian-through-assimilation.

Littlefield, Daniel F. "Cherokee Removal." *The American Mosaic: The
American Indian Experience.* https://americanindian2-abc-clio-
com.ezproxy.liberty.edu/Search/Display/1595705.

Marszalek, John F. "Sherman, William Tecumseh (1820-1891)." *Encyclopedia of
the Great Plains, (2011)* University of Nebraska.
http://plainshumanities.unl.edu/encyclopedia/doc/egp.war.043.

"May 28, 1830 CE: Indian Removal Act."
https://education.nationalgeographic.org/resource/indian-removal-act.

McIver, Stuart. "Bring Me the Head of Osceola." *Sun Sentinel.* https://www.sun-
sentinel.com/news/fl-xpm-1988-01-31-8801070155-story.html.

"Memorial of the Cherokee, 1829."
http://recordsofrights.org/records/39/memorial-of-the-cherokee.

"Native American History Timeline." https://www.history.com/topics/native-
american-history/native-american-timeline.

"Native American Issues Today: Current Problems & Struggles 2022."
http://www.powwows.com/issues-and-problems-facing-native-americans-today.

"Native American Life Today: Understanding the Destruction."
https://pages.nativehope.com/native-americans-today#chp1.

"Native Americans." https://www.mountvernon.org/george-washington/native-
americans/.

Niderost, Eric. "A Massacre of U.S. Soldiers Started the Second Seminole War."
Warfare History Network, (2022) Vol. 22, No. 3.
https://warfarehistorynetwork.com/article/a-massacre-of-u-s-soldiers-started-the-
second-seminole-war/ .

Pauls, Elizabeth Prine. "Trail of Tears" Encyclopedia Britannica, 28 Mar. 2022,
https://www.britannica.com/event/Trail-of-Tears. Accessed 24 August 2022.

Petrini, Andrea R. "The Enlightenment of Thomas Jefferson."
https://elonuniversity.contentdm.oclc.org/digital/collection/p15446coll2/id/11/.

Pruitt, Sarah. "Broken Treaties with Native American Tribes: Timeline." https://www.history.com/news/native-american-broken-treaties.

Pulley, Angela. "Elias Boudinot." *New Georgia Encyclopedia*, 03 September 2002, https://www.georgiaencyclopedia.org/articles/history-archaeology/elias-boudinot-ca-1804-1839/.

"Report of Henry Knox on the Northwestern Indians." https://pages.uoregon.edu/mjdennis/courses/hist469_Knox.htm.

"Seminole History." https://dos.myflorida.com/florida-facts/florida-history/seminole-history/.

"The Creek War of 1836 in Alabama, Georgia, and Florida." https://exploresouthernhistory.com/secondcreekwar.html.

"The Muscogee (Creek) Nation – Legends of America." https://www.legendsofamerica.com/na-creek/.

"The Trail of Tears: They Knew It Was Wrong." Video. https://youtu.be/qalhDKLrWEQ.

"Third Seminole War." https://www.u-s-history.com/pages/h1156.html.

"Trail of Tears: Creek Dissolution." (2002).

Warren, Michael. "Dade's Massacre Reenacts Start of Second Seminole War." https://floridatraveler.com/dades-massacre-recalls-seminole-history/.

Watts, Jennifer. "John Ross: Principal Chief of the Cherokee People." https://tnmuseum.org/junior-curators/posts/john-ross-principal-chief-of-the-cherokee-people?locale=en_us.

"Westward Expansion (1807-1912): Land Policy and Speculation." https://www.sparknotes.com/history/american/westwardexpansion/section2/.